THE FAMILY AND PUBLIC POLICY

Frank F. Furstenberg, Jr., and Andrew J. Cherlin
General Editors

Divided Families

WHAT HAPPENS TO CHILDREN WHEN PARENTS PART

Frank F. Furstenberg, Jr.
Andrew J. Cherlin

Harvard University Press
Cambridge, Massachusetts
London, England · 1991

This book is printed on acid-free paper, and its binding materials
have been chosen for strength and durability.

Library of Congress Cataloging-in-Publication Data
Furstenberg, Frank F., Jr., 1940–
  Divided families : what happens to children when parents part /
Frank F. Furstenberg, Jr., and Andrew J. Cherlin.
    p.   cm.
  Includes index.
  ISBN 0-674-65576-1 (alk. paper)
  1. Children of divorced parents—United States.   2. Divorce—
Economic aspects—United States.   I. Cherlin, Andrew J., 1948–
II. Title.
HQ777.5.F87   1991   90-48171
306.89—dc20   CIP

PREFACE

The publication of *Divided Families* launches a new series sponsored by Harvard University Press on The Family and Public Policy. As the editors of this series and its first authors, we hope to represent in this book a prototype of short volumes by scholars who seek the opportunity to step back from their research and communicate important conclusions to policymakers, practitioners, and the public at large.

Researchers are trained to be cautious about the implications of their studies. Rarely do we believe that the evidence from any single study is sufficient to set public policy, much less guide private decisions. Policymakers and service providers often cannot afford the luxury of waiting for better evidence. This series is aimed at closing the gap between what is known and what should be done about it. We require its authors to draw upon the growing reservoir of social science research to help those who must make difficult choices based on incomplete and sometimes imperfect evidence.

The topic of the social welfare of children has long interested psychologists and students of social welfare, but only recently has it begun to receive the attention it deserves from sociologists, demographers, economists, historians, and legal scholars. These new perspectives, along with the fresh information from developmental psychologists, provide a wealth of empirical evidence on the changing circumstances of families.

This book draws liberally from current research in all of these disciplines to help understand how children are affected by divorce. We have not attempted to summarize research on marital instability but instead to use it to draw judgments about what we can do to help parents and children manage marital disruption and remarriage. Some may find our conclusions controversial and dissent from our reading of the evidence. So much the better if this volume forces readers to bring other evidence to bear on the issues that we have addressed.

A good part of our evidence and much of our understanding about how marital disruption affects children was developed in the course of our own research. Therefore, we must pay a large debt of gratitude to various collaborators who have shared research responsibilities: Paul Allison, Kristin Moore, Phil Morgan, Christine Nord, Jim Peterson, Judy Seltzer, Graham Spanier, and Nicholas Zill. A portion of this book was written while Frank Furstenberg was on leave at the Russell Sage Foundation. The support of the Foundation and especially its president, Eric Wanner, is gratefully acknowledged.

Also, we owe thanks to those who helped us put this book together. Michael Aronson of Harvard University Press inspired and supported this volume and the series of which it is a part. Susan Wallace of the Press contributed sensitive and skilled editorial advice. Patricia Miller deserves credit for her expert administrative, editorial, and clerical services. Kathleen Harris and Judy Levine provided some of the special data runs. Julien Teitler assisted in these and countless other ways, and Connie Blumenthal read the page proofs.

In addition, we benefited a great deal from the comments and criticisms of the members of the W. T. Grant Foundation Divorce Consortium: Gene H. Brody, Kathleen A. Camara, Robert E. Emery, Rex Forehand, E. Mavis Hetherington, Eleanor Maccoby, Robert Mnookin, Joanne Pedro-Carroll, Lonnie Sherrod, Donald Wertlieb, and Nicholas Zill. Irv Garfinkel read and commented on the manuscript as well.

CONTENTS

Divided Families

CHAPTER 1

Divorce and the American Family

At the beginning of this century, when our grandparents were marrying, getting divorced was a rare event and a serious moral transgression. In the 1930s, when our parents married, divorce was still uncommon and remained a social disgrace. Divorce was not so unusual by the time we wed. Even so, Americans remained convinced that divorce should only occur under desperate conditions and that society should not make it easy for couples to break their bonds. Today, as our children contemplate marriage, divorce is commonplace. It is now regarded as an unfortunate but inevitable risk of entering into a marriage.

Although Americans still cling to the ideal that marriage should be a life-long commitment, most couples, even as they stand hand-and-hand at the altar, now recognize the possibility that their marriage might not work out. Of course, they will tell you that they are fully prepared to work hard to stay together. But they will probably also tell you that people who are unhappy in marriage should not stay together—not even for the sake of the children. In 1962 when a sample of young mothers were asked whether couples with children ought to remain together if they could not get along, half said they should. But when these same women were asked the identical question in 1985, fewer than one in five said they should.[1] There are no public-opinion data about how our grandparents and great-grandparents would have answered such a question. Yet even if public-opinion polls existed at the turn of the century, probably no one would have thought to ask whether it was all right for unhappy couples to end their marriages. Emotional discontent was not a reason for getting divorced, especially if children were involved. Naturally, some people ignored the prevailing social mores; but when they did, they were treated as outcasts.

If you look around today, it is possible to find local communities in this country where divorce is still strongly condemned. Divorce is unusual among Mennonites and causes a stir among Mormons, religious Catholics, and Orthodox Jews. For most Americans, however, ending a marriage is a matter of personal choice. Family and friends may mourn the breakup of a longstanding marriage, but they hardly ever denounce the parties involved. This is not to say that Americans are oblivious to the consequences of divorce for children. Many of us recognize that children often are the casualties of this new marriage system, in which parents get to choose new partners. We feel uneasy about how this system is working out for children. At the same time, we don't quite know what to do about it.

We hope this book will help readers to understand better what happens to children and their parents during and after a divorce. People mistakenly think of divorce as an event that occurs all at once: a judge signs a decree, and a married couple instantly become divorced. But divorce is actually a process that starts long before the couple's day in court. It begins with a troubled marriage and proceeds—often two steps forward, one step back—to an end when one parent leaves home for good. Physically apart, the estranged spouses still face the difficult and often painful tasks of separating emotionally, economically, and legally. They also must establish ways to care for and support their children. The date the divorce becomes final is almost incidental; most people can't even recall it.

In Chapter 2 we describe what typically happens during this process of uncoupling. We note the impact on children as their parents move further apart, and we examine the new forms of parenting that emerge. How parents manage the process, many believe, affects children's later adjustment. In Chapter 3 we tell the distressing story of the economic slide of mothers and children after divorce and look into why it occurs. Chapter 4 reports the wide variations in the impact of divorce on children's development and well-being.

For many parents, the process of divorce leads to a remarriage, an event that once more changes the face of the family's daily life. Children must adjust to a stepparent and often to a bewildering array of steprelatives; how well they do so is discussed in Chapter 5. Finally, in Chapter 6, we examine how our society might respond to the great rise in divorce. We consider whether it is possible—or desirable—for our government to take steps to strengthen marriage. We ask whether there are actions that can reduce the level of divorce or, if not, can lessen its harmful effects. We consider ways to help single parents cope with the demands of work and children. What measures, we ask, ought to have top priority? What further changes should be made in the law? How much can we expect of fathers? It is with these difficult questions of public policy that we will close this book.

This first chapter provides some background for understanding how and why this transformation in our marriage system came about. Some people still hope that we may return to the days when divorce was uncommon. In explaining why changes in marriage took place, we'll try to say why this return is unlikely to happen. The second part of this chapter reviews some of the facts and figures on marital disruption. Until quite recently, sociologists who studied the family focused mainly on adults. Now demographers and sociologists are bringing children into the picture. As they do, they are seeing that family disruption looks very different when viewed through a child's eyes. Our aim is to use some of the most recent demographic data to construct a clear picture of the family changes that children are likely to experience—what we call the life course of children of divorce. Not all children are equally likely to be caught up in family flux; the odds of encountering marital disruption and remarriage during the course of childhood vary greatly. What happens to children after their parents divorce also differs. These variations in the life course of children of divorce help us to understand why children react so differently to what at first glance seem to be similar events.

OUR CHANGING MARRIAGE SYSTEM

How Americans managed to change their ideas about marriage so profoundly in the course of this century is the subject of a good deal of scholarly investigation and academic debate. Yet no one fully understands how divorce became such a widely accepted part of our marriage system. Even saying that divorce is a part of our marriage system may strike some readers as a strange idea. We are accustomed to thinking of divorce not as an intrinsic part of our marriage system but as a sign that the system is not working well. Suppose, however, that anthropologists completely unfamiliar with the U.S. population came to study the marriage customs of our "tribe." These observers would immediately notice that many marriages end in divorce. Just by talking to people, reading the newspapers, and watching television or movies, they would see that Americans do not speak about marriage without also speaking of divorce. And they would find that our legal system has established procedures for dissolving marriages, dividing property, and sharing responsibility for the children. How could these anthropologists not conclude that divorce is deeply embedded in the American kinship system? How could they fail to see that laws and customs define marriage as a voluntary contract that can be dissolved at the discretion of either party?

Some scholars trace the voluntary and discretionary features of our marriage system far back in time. The roots of the "divorce revolution," as Lenore Weitzman has called it, can be found in what the historian Lawrence Stone identified as the rise of affective individualism in early modern England: a greater emphasis on emotional bonds among the members of the nuclear family and on the individual pursuit of happiness. Another historian, Edward Shorter, claims that Americans have always displayed a stronger preference for emotional gratification in family relations and a relatively lower tolerance for the obligations of kinship than the more traditional cultures of Western Europe.[2]

Compared with many Europeans, Americans may have embraced "the romantic love complex" early in our history, giving more weight to personal and emotional considerations in the marriage choice and less weight to family influence. By the early nineteenth century, long before divorce was socially acceptable, marriage was defined as more of a personal than a family decision.[3] To be sure, families maintained a protective presence; but they at best exercised veto rights. In the twentieth century, they were consulted less and less. Increasingly, marriage resulted from "falling in love," a practice that undermined the exercise of parental control.[4]

Throughout much of the twentieth century, being in love was seen as the standard for entering marriage but not for maintaining marriage. Until the early 1960s, a central issue in the sociological literature on the family was how people moved beyond love to marriage. Romantic love was considered a dangerous recipe for matrimonial success.[5] The challenge for young couples was to revise unrealistic illusions of emotional gratification formed in courtship to mature, albeit less passionate, feelings of companionship. If they were sometimes disappointed in the conversion of love to marriage, young couples at least could be sure that many others were in the same boat.

In retrospect, it is easy to see that the fault lines in our marriage system were gradually widening throughout this century. But the cracks did not become clear until the early 1960s, when the divorce rate began to rise so sharply that it doubled by the mid-1970s. Why did this gigantic jump occur? Perhaps the most important reason was the growing number of married women who were working outside the home and the change in gender relations this trend produced. This is not to say that the rise in female employment directly accounted for the surge of divorce. Rather, the entrance of women into the labor force is at the core of a constellation of changes in the American family that has caused both men and women to rethink marriage.[6]

As the nation industrialized from the middle of the nineteenth to the middle of the twentieth century, married men increasingly found employment outside the home, whereas their wives remained at home. Of course, women frequently were gainfully employed at home, taking in boarders or doing odd jobs, and they were often engaged in productive activities that directly contributed to the economic welfare of the family. But over time, job opportunities for women outside the home became more attractive relative to what they could produce at home. The rise of the service sector of the economy created a demand for educated workers that employers filled by hiring women as secretaries, teachers, and nurses. And during the same period, families began to have fewer children as they moved from the farm—where children could help out from an early age—to the city. So women were needed less at home and had better opportunities to work for wages (even though their wages remained far below men's).

The result was a slow but steady movement of married women into the labor market. As recently as 1940, just one in seven married women was working outside the home.[7] During the 1950s, married women whose children all had reached school age began to work in larger numbers. And starting in the 1960s, increasing numbers of married women with children under age six began to work outside the home.

The entry of married women into the work force broke down a division of labor in the family that was much celebrated as recently as the 1950s: the single-earner, two-parent, breadwinner-homemaker family. Although often labeled as traditional, it was a modern creation. Its emergence reflected the growth of wage labor among husbands during early industrialization. Its demise, which reflected the much later growth of wage labor among wives, had profound consequences for married life. As gender roles within marriage have become less distinct, the benefits of marriage have become less obvious. Men, some say, don't have as good a deal as they once did.[8] They are not as willing to bear the obligations of family life because they are less likely to enjoy their traditional privileges—deference and domestic support.[9] For their part, women are not as willing to endure an unsatisfactory relationship if they can support themselves. So emotional gratification has become the *sine qua non* of married life. It is the main glue that holds couples together.

During the same period that women were entering the work force in ever larger numbers, attitudes toward divorce were becoming more tolerant. The changes in divorce laws in the 1960s and 1970s, most notably the elimination of the need to prove that one partner was at fault, signaled the end of a battle that had been waged for more than a century over the social acceptability of divorce.[10] Until then, divorced persons were stigmatized and viewed as morally suspect. In the 1950s Adlai Stevenson was hampered in his run for the Presidency by a divorce. In the 1980s, no one cared about Ronald Reagan's divorce.

Part of the process of normalizing a social practice like divorce is the construction of new and different public images. Throughout the 1960s and 1970s, divorced persons became more visible in the mass media. They were portrayed more sympathetically—or, better yet, in the ultimate form of acceptance, they were portrayed indifferently. Think about how Americans now regard cohabitation, compared with the strong reaction to it a decade or two ago. That change is similar to what happened to divorce in the 1960s and 1970s. Attitude change is partly a circular process. Behavior influences public attitudes, which in turn influence behavior.

Why, then, did the divorce rate double? Economists like to say that there is less to exchange in marriage.[11] They are right. When emotions are the primary, if not exclusive, currency of exchange in marriage, you can begin to see why divorce becomes more prevalent. Sociologists like to say that the moral constraints that discourage divorce are weaker. They are right, too. There is less social pressure on couples to stay married. To be sure, some couples will stay together out of a sense of obligation to each other or to their children, but fewer and fewer are inclined to stay together for that reason alone. Marriage has become a choice rather than a necessity, a one-dimensional institution sustained almost exclusively by emotional satisfaction, and difficult to maintain in its absence.

DIVORCE INVOLVES CHILDREN

But people get married in part because they want to have children. And when they decide to divorce, children are frequently left in the lurch. A major reason for writing this book is to weigh the costs of divorce to children and to explore how these costs might be minimized. Still, it probably does not help children who may be disadvantaged by our current marriage practices to lament the passing of the family of bygone days. Keep in mind, too, that we are inclined to romanticize the virtues and overlook the weaknesses of so-called

8   traditional families. Historians who have looked closely at family life in earlier centuries observe that many children did not have it so good. Until well into the twentieth century, mortality and disease ravaged many families.[12] Even today, despite the rise in divorce, children are far more likely to spend their childhood living with at least one parent than they were a century ago—because adult death rates are so much lower.[13]

Historians also have their doubts about whether children were better protected and cared for by their parents in earlier eras. In his controversial account of the premodern family, Edward Shorter characterizes family life in the past as "the bad old days." He claims that parents—faced with the continual stresses of economic uncertainty, illness, and natural disasters—often neglected, exploited, and even abused their offspring.[14] To be sure, not everyone agrees with this Dickensian portrait of family life in earlier times.[15] Shorter probably overstates his case and, in any event, concedes that the American family was more "modern" in its childrearing attitudes than most of Western Europe.

Whether children were cared for by their parents more or less conscientiously a century ago is not really answerable. Our standards of what is proper and desirable parental supervision have changed radically in the interim, making it difficult to draw comparisons. And even if we could, the data are simply too fragmentary to provide convincing assessments. We suspect that Americans are more worried about the welfare of children than perhaps ever before in our history. But this public display of concern does not necessarily imply that children are worse off now than they ever were. Based on the best information available, our guess is that most children receive more love and affection today and probably no less supervision than they did in previous centuries. If we are correct, then why all the fuss?

We would argue that whereas children may be no worse off today than a century ago, very possibly they are worse off than they were thirty or forty years ago. For most Americans, this more recent comparison is the relevant one. Many of us can remember the 1950s, a time when the adolescent years seemed to be relatively benign by today's standards. To be sure, the portrait of youth in the 1950s was not entirely positive. Observers worried about rising rates of delinquency, promiscuity, and alienation. At the same time, social critics complained about the over-conformity of youth and the lack of a rebellious response to social institutions.[16] But the level of apprehension was nowhere near as high as it is now. Few worried about poverty, child abuse, dropping out of school, drug use, suicide, runaways, teenage childbearing, and the rest of the litany of social problems that are associated with growing up today.[17]

These problems all appear to be on the rise, and some experts believe that the reasons for the rise are the sharp increases in family instability and in mothers working outside the home. Parents, it is argued, don't seem as involved in caring for their children as they were in the 1950s, when the breadwinner-homemaker family prevailed. The disintegration of family life, popular writers like Marie Winn tell us, has liberated adults from the central obligation of parenthood—the supervision of their children.[18] Out-of-control and permissive parents, these writers argue, have produced a generation of problem children.

In the chapters that follow we will examine the evidence on the consequences of divorce in some detail and will demonstrate that the picture is more complex than these writers acknowledge. But as a prelude, it is useful to become better acquainted with the way that the increase in divorce has altered the process of growing up in families.

THE LIFE COURSE OF CHILDREN OF DIVORCE

The best way to appreciate the changes in children's experience with divorce is to compare children's family circumstances in different historical eras. Suppose we were to look at three prototypical cohorts of children, each born about a half century apart, in 1900, 1950, and 1990. These dates correspond, respectively, to periods when divorce was still relatively rare, when it was more common but not yet prevalent, and finally when it had become widespread. Although it is difficult to make accurate estimates, we doubt that more than 7 or 8 percent of children in 1900 lost a parent through separation or divorce before reaching late adolescence.[19]

Remember, however, that children born in 1900 still had a much higher risk of losing a parent through death. The demographer Peter Uhlenberg has estimated that almost a quarter of all children born at the beginning of this century lost at least one parent by death by age fifteen.[20] So if the effects of death and divorce are considered jointly, the amount of family instability in the early 1900s was quite high. Perhaps as many as one out of three children lived in a single-parent family at some point, usually because their mother or father died during their childhood.

By mid-century, circumstances had changed dramatically because of declining death rates. Larry L. Bumpass and James A. Sweet have estimated that only 5 percent of children born in the 1950s lost a parent by death. But divorce rates had increased, and about 11 percent of children experienced the separation or divorce of their parents. Furthermore, another 6 percent were born to unmarried parents.[21] So if we add the percentage of children who lost a parent by death to the percentage who lost a parent through separation or divorce and to the percentage whose parents weren't married, the total comes to 22 percent. This total is substantially lower than the level of family disruption that occurred a half-century earlier, when approximately a third of all children lived with a single parent at some point.

But the reduction in children's experience with family disruption lasted only a decade. To be sure, mortality rates continued to decline from their already low levels, but rates of voluntary marital disruption rose sharply from the early 1960s to the mid-1970s. In addition, from the 1960s onward a growing proportion of children have been born to unmarried parents. At first, this trend was just a trickle (although it has long been a substantial fraction of black children). But the trickle has grown to a steady stream in recent years. In 1987, 24 percent of all births occurred out of wedlock, compared with just 4 percent in 1950.[22] The mother and father of some of these children will eventually marry each other, but postnuptial marriages between unmarried parents are probably becoming less common; and, when they do occur, they seem to be occurring later in the child's life. Thus, a growing percentage of children are being raised by a single parent (almost always the child's mother) because their parents never marry or delay marriage.

When the risks of unmarried parenthood are added to the risks of divorce, the proportion of children spending at least part of their childhood growing up in a single-parent family is truly staggering. Bumpass and Sweet estimate that 44 percent of children born between 1970 and 1984 will live in a single-parent family before age sixteen.[23] We would guess that for children born in the 1990s, the figure could reach 60 percent if the divorce rate remains high and nonmarital childbearing continues its upward trend. Indeed, if childbearing outside of marriage—in informal, temporary, or casual unions—becomes any more common, then calculating marital stability will become less and less meaningful. A growing number of "marriages" will be unregistered events or nonevents.*

We will not be able to give much attention in this book to children whose parents never marry, or even to those who live in informal unions that subsequently break up. Until quite recently, children who spent their entire lives in single-parent families were extremely rare; they are still uncommon. Consequently, the scholarly research on this special group is inadequate. Most of what researchers know comes from studies of teenage childbearing and studies of black family life. But even most teenage mothers until quite recently have married while their children were young.[24] Researchers have not yet sorted out the relative effects of nonmarital childbearing and separation and divorce.[25] Moreover, the process of marital disruption introduces different kinds of concerns for children than those which result from unmarried parenthood. Specifically, divorce involves a transition from a two-parent to a single-parent household. Some of our later discussion, particularly when we describe the economic issues associated with life in a single-parent family, the problems of

*This trend obviously creates some consternation among social scientists who are interested in measuring marital disruption and its impact on children. The official rate of disruption could actually go down while the unofficial rate is rising. The more selective people become about whether or not to marry, the more difficult it will be to tell if marital stability is changing. Suppose, as may have already happened in some European nations, only those couples who have strong religious scruples elect to marry. The divorce rate could drop only because the people who are electing to marry are quite different from those who choose to live in informal unions or not marry at all. This makes it difficult, to say the least, to track the stability of marriage, not to mention our topic—the consequences of divorce for children.

child support, and policy alternatives for increasing paternal involvement, applies to children of unmarried as well as previously married parents. When appropriate we will make these similarities explicit, but we are generally limiting ourselves to what we know about the effects of marital dissolution on children.

DIVORCE IS ONLY A TRANSITIONAL EVENT

We face another complication in charting the experiences of children growing up today. Not only has marriage become less predictable and less stable, but marital careers have become more complex. We use the term *career* to signify the growing number of adults who move through a sequence of marital arrangements. If these individuals happen to be parents, their children will be transported with them from one union to the next. Viewed from the children's perspective, marital disruption is not the end but the beginning of a series of family changes. Demographers who try to portray the family experiences of children are scratching their heads, wondering how to capture the complex life course that many children born in the 1980s and 1990s will follow.

Two examples will illustrate this dilemma. One of these studies traced the lives of children born to teenage mothers in the mid-1960s in Baltimore.[26] Most participants in the study were black, many were poor or near-poor, and most had spent their entire lives in the city of Baltimore. The majority of the teen mothers in the study eventually married, often to the father of their child, although about a fifth never married at all.

Consider one of the children, Theo, who lived for two years with her mother and grandmother before her parents started living together. When she was three, they married; but her father moved out just before her sixth birthday. When Theo was eight, her mother started living with Robbie, who became like a stepfather to Theo until he moved out when she was fifteen. Throughout her childhood, Theo has continued to see her biological father on an occasional basis, though these visits have become more and more irregular. After Robbie left, he, too, continued to visit Theo and her half-brother, who was his biological child. Still another surrogate father lived with Theo for a brief time after her quasi-stepfather Robbie moved out, but this relationship was short-lived and of little consequence. It's difficult to calculate the usual demographic statistics for Theo's childhood. How many years did she spend in a single-parent household? How many times did she experience "marital disruption"? It is even more difficult to think about which of her "fathers" has an obligation to contribute to her support in her late adolescent years now that she is living with only her mother.

Theo's family experience, while more complex than most, was not unusual among the children in the Baltimore study. Only a small percentage grew up with both biological parents in the house. The children in the Baltimore study typically had relationships with at least two father figures; and it was not uncommon to have several surrogate fathers. To be sure, the offspring of teen mothers are an extreme case. They are at one end of a continuum, at the other end of which are children who spend their entire childhood in the same family situation. Not so long ago the children who lived in stable, two-biological-parent households were in the majority. But this may no longer be true. And an increasing number of American children are growing up in circumstances that resemble Theo's life course.

A second example is a boy, Vincent, who participated in the National Survey of Children, a representative sample of children that has been followed from the mid-1970s to the present. Vincent's parents married several years before he was born and did not separate until he was nearly seven. After his parents' divorce, Vincent lived with his mother and his grandmother for a time. Then his mother moved in with a man who eventually became Vincent's stepfather. This second marriage lasted for almost four years, after which it, too, dissolved. Now Vincent's mom is living on and off with a new partner, and it is not clear whether or not she will marry again.

There are other youth like Vincent in the National Survey of Children. If this same study were to be redone today, there would be even more children who lived in two or more family situations during childhood. Well over a third of the youth in the National Survey of Children witnessed the breakup of their parents' marriage before they reached the age of sixteen, and another 10 percent or so experienced life in a single-parent family because their parents were unmar-

14 ried or because of the death of a parent. Like Vincent, most of those whose parents divorced eventually entered a stepfamily. Roughly one child in five acquired at least one stepparent before turning eighteen. For children growing up in the 1980s and 1990s, the probability of acquiring a stepparent will be even higher. Perhaps one out of every four will enter a stepfamily by their late teens. In addition, others, like Theo and Vincent, will have the experience of living in a household with a quasi-stepparent because of the growing prevalence of cohabitation both before marriage and after divorce.

But many of the children whose parents remarry will share Vincent's fate. Their new family will not last. The rate of marital disruption among remarried parents is even greater than the rate of disruption among parents in their first marriages. A third of all the children in the National Survey of Children whose parents remarried saw their parents get divorced again by the time the children were in early adolescence. That figure rose to nearly half by the time the children reached their late teens. If these rates of redivorce hold for the current crop of children, and it seems almost certain that they will, approximately 15 percent of all children will see their custodial parent divorce, remarry, and redivorce before they reach the age of eighteen. A portion of this group will have even more complex family lives as their parents either marry again or enter informal unions. These estimates account only for the experiences of the children's custodial parents, leaving uncounted the family transitions of noncustodial parents. The children who continue to see their other parent outside the home may acquire still another stepparent and possibly a set of new siblings. Children who have family lives like Theo and Vincent will not be so unusual in the 1990s.

Although white children are far less likely to encounter marital disruption during their lifetime than are black children, the National Survey of Children tells us that white youth are much more likely to enter stepfamilies. They were more than twice as likely as black children to acquire stepparents and were therefore at greater risk of experiencing a second disruption. Black children more often than whites never live with their biological father and certainly spend less time living with a father figure of any kind. Keep in mind, however, that the figures for blacks as well as whites excluded informal marital arrangements and may therefore underestimate the true level of family flux. Family instability for both whites and blacks is rapidly becoming the rule rather than the exception.

As we've said, these shifting states make it extremely difficult to describe the family life of children today, much less to measure the effects of particular family arrangements on the developing child. But the important point is that a huge number of children are likely to experience complex family lives in response to their parent's complex family careers. Certainly, compared with the 1950s and even with the early decades of this century, family life has become more variable and less predictable for children. Whatever the advantages of the new marriage system for parents, it has introduced a great deal of uncertainty in the family lives of America's children.

A CONCLUDING NOTE

If it is any comfort, the situation in the United States is far from unique. Marriage and divorce trends, and many of the family changes which we have depicted in this chapter, have occurred in virtually all Western nations over the past several decades. Just as in this country, in a number of European countries divorce rates have soared since the mid-1960s. In Belgium, France, and Switzerland rates have doubled, while in Canada, England, and the Netherlands they have risen threefold.[27] Even though the United States still outranks all other nations by a considerable margin, the cross-national differentials are diminishing. (And if dissolutions of informal, cohabiting unions were counted, Sweden and possibly Denmark would have rates comparable to the United States.) With few exceptions, most developed societies are undergoing the same sort of family transformation that has occurred in this country. To say that, throughout the Western world, almost every nation has experienced a shift toward a more voluntaristic marriage system is not to say that every country has responded to these changes in the same way. Later on, we will look at some of the fascinating differences in countries' responses to the dilemmas that marital disruption creates for children. But our first task is to see how Americans manage the process of divorce and remarriage.

CHAPTER 2

When Marriages Come Apart

We cannot hope to make sense of how children are affected by divorce unless we also examine what happens to their parents as they go through a marital transition or, often, a sequence of marital transitions. Unfortunately, most research either describes the process of divorce from the parents' or the child's perspective—not both at once. More often than not, sociologists specialize in describing the process of divorce for adults, while psychologists specialize in children's experiences. Yet, the best studies have deliberately crossed these artificial disciplinary boundaries to show that what happens to children after divorce can be largely understood by how their parents go about divorcing. There are better and worse ways of ending marriages, at least when it comes to protecting the interests of children.

Throughout this book we are going to follow a typical case of a divorcing couple. Though not an actual couple, Herb and Helen are like many couples that we and other researchers have studied as they go through a divorce. What happens to them and their two children, Mickey and Sally, will illustrate many of the common dilemmas that families face when parents part.

During their eight-year marriage Herb and Helen had gotten along poorly for most of the time. Helen complained that Herb was emotionally remote, was stingy with his affections, and constantly ridiculed her family. As her complaints grew more insistent, Herb withdrew into his close circle of male companions—the guys that he had grown up with from childhood. Helen, in his view, had become a nag who had no sense of humor and didn't know how to enjoy herself. Despite their ungratifying marriage, neither Herb nor Helen ever thought seriously about getting divorced. Both had come from stable families where divorce was rare. Moreover, their families were acquainted with one another and had urged them to work out their difficulties.

However, the fighting grew severe just before their first child was born. On the advice of her sister-in-law, Helen visited a therapist. Herb refused to go, but he did listen more carefully to Helen's complaints. For a while, their relationship improved. But the fighting started up again two years later just before Helen's second pregnancy. After their daughter was born, their relations deteriorated badly and the fighting became almost constant. Mickey, who had been an easy-going toddler, became more difficult. Helen, worried about his behavior, recognized that the marriage was taking its toll, not only on her but also on their son. Helen insisted that she and Herb either seek counseling or that Herb move out. Herb, agreeing that the fighting was not good for Mickey, decided to try separating for a while.

Only when Herb finally moved out did the children learn of their parents' problems. Even then, both parents continued to reassure the children that they would probably get back together. In fact, they did reunite for nearly a month but then separated again for good. During the eighteen-month period between the separation and the divorce, Herb saw his children several times a week. And after the divorce was finalized, he continued to see them regularly for the next year or so. But then his contact began to drop off sharply. Several years after the divorce, he saw his son only a few times a month and his daughter even less often.

The pattern exhibited by Herb and Helen is quite common. When marriages end, relatively few couples are able to continue to cooperate in raising their children. Generally, fathers pull away or are discouraged—sometimes by their former wife, sometimes by a new woman in their life—from staying involved with their children. Mothers usually wind up with the responsibility for the kids. The absence of fathers from the family has profound consequences for children's economic well-being and possibly their psychological well-being, too. This chapter tries to describe and explain the process by which most marriages come apart.

Part of the explanation involves the connection in our culture between marriage and childrearing. Families are designed to manage these two separate but related activities at once. In the recent past, marriage and parenthood were welded together so smoothly that the seams hardly showed at all. People generally got married only when they were prepared to have children, and they only had children when they were married. In fact, a few decades ago several leading authorities on American kinship claimed that a family was really a family only when a married couple had children.[1]

Sociologists now like to point out that the role of a husband or wife is distinctly different from the role of mother or father. Yet most married couples with children don't separate their marriage and parenting duties. Mom and Dad don't submit separate time sheets for marriage credit or child-care credit when they cook a meal, fix a light plug, or go off to work in the morning. This works fine until Mom and Dad decide not to live together. When this happens, couples are forced to sort and separate their marital and childrearing roles. This surgical procedure turns out to be difficult. Indeed, the inability of parents to manage the separation of marriage and parenthood is at the root of many of the problems that children experience after divorce. It seems that many parents only know how to be parents when they are married and living together. So when the marriage breaks up, all too often the baby (and the baby's older brothers and sisters) gets thrown out with the bath water.

Part of the problem has to do simply with the ill will generated by the ending of an intimate relationship. Given the high premium we Americans place on intimacy in marriage, the emotional trauma surrounding the breakup is understandable. Many divorced parents are too angry or hurt to cooperate in childrearing with their ex-spouses. In addition, men and women usually experience divorce quite differently because they have invested differently in their marriages. These separate ways of looking at marriage and divorce, as we shall see, greatly complicate achieving a viable child-care arrangement after separation.

HOW COUPLES SEPARATE

From a very early age, most Americans can tell you a lot about falling in love and getting married. How people fall out of love and exit from marriage is a more mysterious process. Like courtship, marital dissolution follows what social scientists call a natural history; that is, most individuals pass through a series of predictable stages on the way to ending their marriages.[2] Couples face common problems in disengaging and often therefore arrive at common solutions. Although this process of uncoupling may not follow a completely orderly form, it is like the course of an illness (or a recovery), during which couples move from being husband and wife to being ex-spouses.

During this process, the formerly married partners must pass through various "stations," to use Paul Bohannan's term for the essential tasks of divorce.[3] They must make an emotional separation, work out legal arrangements, divide their economic assets, come to some agreement about how to continue their parenting responsibilities, renegotiate relations with their respective families, and become reintegrated into the larger community as unmarried persons. This process divides what was a social, psychological, and legal entity into its constituent parts. Yet we have no cultural guidelines, no standard procedures, for telling couples when and how to exit from a marriage that is not working out. Herb and Helen's case is like many others. The problems in their marriage began long before they thought a lot about breaking up. Helen was more openly discontented, but she was reluctant to give up on the marriage. Herb acknowledged that there were problems, although he never thought they were quite as bad as Helen did. He would have stayed married if Helen hadn't pushed him for a greater emotional commitment. But eventually, Herb, too, had to admit that they were quarreling almost constantly and that neither really cared for the other. Mild dissatisfaction eventually turned to enmity.

In one study of divorcing couples in central Pennsylvania, nearly half the women who ultimately separated said that they had thought about the possibility for at least two years before taking any concrete actions. The men in the study typically had a shorter separation process or perhaps were simply less conscious of serious problems in their marriage. This finding is consistent with many other studies showing that perceptions of marital distress follow traditional gender patterns: women tend to be more attuned to emotional discontents, and men are usually more oblivious or deny the shortcomings of an impoverished emotional relationship.[4] Perhaps it is only that women expect more emotionally from marriage than men and are therefore less tolerant of what some sociologists have called an empty-shell marriage.[5]

It is difficult to say just how long it takes couples to make the transition out of marriage. Many formerly married couples cannot even agree on when their marriages began to break up. How would we actually date the end of Herb and Helen's marriage? Would it be when they first decided to separate, when they actually first parted, or when the second separation occurred? Like Herb and Helen, many couples separate and get back together again, sometimes doing so several times before the final collapse of their marriage.[6]

The length of the separation process is highly variable. At one extreme are the unusual instances in which one partner discovers that the marriage is over by reading a note left on the kitchen table. Such a sudden announcement does not happen as often when children are involved. At the other extreme are those marriages that take fifteen or twenty years to dissolve. Most often, the terminal period of marriages—the time between the onset of serious difficulties and the final separation—usually lasts several years. Contrary to popular stereotype, most couples, especially those with children, do not relinquish their marital bonds easily or with little cause.

Some of the best statistical data on the process of divorce comes from the National Survey of Children (NSC), the study mentioned in the previous chapter that followed families with children over time. In 1981, the custodial parents of some 300 children from separated and divorced families in the sample were asked a number of retrospective questions about the dissolution of their marriages. This subgroup is of particular interest to us because all the informants had children, and many had been in longstanding marriages.[7] Keep in mind that the informants are mostly women who had separated, on average, five years before. Nonetheless, their accounts seem to match fairly well with other studies of the separation process.[8]

Was the divorce anticipated? (Of real interest to us is whether children might have received some advanced warning of the impending disruption of their parents' marriage.) More than a quarter (28 percent) of the couples had often discussed the possibility of divorce before separating; another 39 percent had talked about it at least occasionally. Still, a third of the couples had not openly considered the possibility of the marriage's breaking up before it actually happened—a disturbingly large proportion who had done no prior planning. Many couples begin the process of separation undecided about its ultimate outcome. They test the water, often by a trial separation which may or may not be permanent. Half the participants in the NSC reported going through one or more temporary separations before their marriage finally ended. The unraveling of these marriages usually extended over a period of some months, often some years, leaving their children in a prolonged period of uncertainty and confusion.

This period when marriages come apart is often a time of severe marital strife, sometimes culminating in physical conflict. Half the respondents (56 percent) recalled frequent fighting prior to the separation, and most of the rest (29 percent) remembered fighting at least occasionally. Of those who ever fought, more than a third said that these fights sometimes became physical. One in five stated that they had been seriously injured or abused on at least one occasion. These data square with the reports of other investigators which show that physical abuse is common in dissolving marriages. For example, in the best-known clinical study of divorce, Wallerstein and Kelly write about the separation process, "Not surprisingly, there was a good deal of anger, resulting in physical abuse—usually by men of their wives—or property destruction, accompanied by a good deal of fear."[9] Another clinically based investigation reported even higher levels of physical violence among divorcing parents than we observed in the NSC. And this study discovered that when instances of aggression occurred, children were present two thirds of the time.[10]

Given the extended period of conflict preceding the dissolution of most marriages, we might expect that both partners would be ready to end the relationship by the time one leaves. But the data suggest otherwise. Four out of five marriages ended unilaterally, usually at the wife's insistence. A number of researchers have speculated that men frequently provoke their wives into insisting on a divorce, thus relieving them of the responsibility for dissolving the marriage.[11]

To sum up, despite the wide variability in the way that couples end their relationships, some measure of regularity exists in the separation process. Usually, it takes couples quite a while to relinquish their bonds, and the end rarely comes easily. When it finally does, it is generally women who decide to call it quits. In the end it was Helen who gave Herb an ultimatum to shape up or move out. She kept hoping that their relations would improve, but she felt she could not endure the way they were. Women like Helen feel compelled to act. But the men often see themselves as being kicked out of the house. This split along gender lines often has consequences for the postmarital relations between men and women and for the involvement of fathers in the family after the marriage dissolves.

CHILDREN AND THE SEPARATION PROCESS

When Herb and Helen split up, Sally was really too young to understand what was going on. Mickey, however, had suspicions even before Herb moved out for the first time. "Why are you and Daddy not liking each other?" he asked his mother repeatedly in the year before the separation occurred. Helen tried to be reassuring but was deliberately vague in her response. "Even when we don't get along, Daddy and I both still love you and Sally. We will always be a family." She intended to say that Mickey should not worry even if his parents' marriage did not survive. In fact, Helen was worried about this herself, and her elliptical attempts at reassuring Mickey were hardly effective.

The first time that Herb moved out, he explained to the children that he had to go away because Mommy and he were not getting along and needed to "fix their relationship." When he moved back, Mickey asked him if the relationship was fixed. Herb gave Mickey a hug and suggested that they go out for ice cream. Just before Herb moved out for good a month later, he and Helen talked to Mickey, explaining that they had been unable to fix their relationship. Both parents promised that they would still be a "family." "Do you understand that?" Helen asked her son. Mickey nodded, but he didn't really see how they could be a family when his father was living somewhere else.

Divorce is confusing to most children, even children a lot older than Mickey. The NSC was a survey, not a clinical study. For this reason children were not directly asked to provide their perceptions of the divorce process. In any case, many, like Sally, were too young at the time to have had much of a recollection. Nevertheless, we can infer from the adults' accounts how their children learned about the separation. The parents were asked how much the child knew about their marital difficulties before the breakup occurred. According to the parents, a third of the children were completely aware. Another third described Herb and Helen's situation: the children were aware that the parents were getting along badly but were only dimly aware that they might part. This still leaves a substantial minority who were in the dark (although some of this uninformed children were undoubtedly too young to be able to perceive what was happening).

It may be obvious to most children prior to a divorce that their parents are getting along badly. Still, like Mickey, relatively few are forewarned of the possibility of an impending separation. About a third of the children in the NSC were given advance notice of a month or more; most of the others learned either just before (12 percent) or not until after (28 percent) one parent moved out. The rest, according to the parents, were too young to be told, although most were in fact preschoolers capable of understanding some sort of explanation. Wallerstein and Kelly reported a similar result in their study of divorcing families. They found that "fully one-third of the children had only a brief awareness of their parent's unhappiness prior to the divorce decision." Among the youngest children, the warning time was even shorter. "Four-fifths of the youngest children studied were not provided with . . . an adequate explanation . . . In effect, they awoke one morning to find one parent gone."[12]

The reticence of parents to inform their children of the impending separation is quite understandable, even though it may have unfortunate repercussions later on. As has been noted, some of the parents themselves were caught by surprise when a spouse abruptly left. Others, like Herb and Helen, faced an ambiguous and fluid situation. They were not, themselves, certain that their marriage was coming apart. Separation is often an unplanned, if not entirely unforeseen, event. Many parents therefore are not in a position to keep their children apprised of their changing state of affairs. Still others believe, as Herb and Helen did, that premature discussions with their children would likely do more harm than good.

Most children, then, only learn about the separation when it is a fait accompli. Even then, they are likely to receive a fuzzy account of what is going on. In many cases, their parents are unsure themselves. When Mickey asked his mother after the initial separation, "When is Daddy coming back?" Helen could only reply, "I'm not sure." Then she added, mostly for Mickey's sake but in part for herself, "Soon, I hope."

If this uncertainty for parents is difficult, it is much more so for children, who cannot imagine a family life other than the one that they have had. We don't know for certain whether or not children such as Mickey and his sister would have been better off in the long run if they had been given more advance warning. Many clinicians believe that the failure of parents to communicate with their children adds to the immediate burden of the divorce for children and contributes to the children's sense of uncertainty. However, no amount of preparation could help children comprehend the painful events that often follow a parent's departure from the home.

WHEN SEPARATION OCCURS

If the process leading up to the separation is ambiguous and ill-defined, so too is the process of establishing separate households. It might seem that the intrusion of the legal system would reduce the variation in how divorcing couples behave after they cease to live together. After all, couples must eventually reach a separation agreement, which defines the rights and responsibilities of each partner in the wake of the marriage. But the order imposed by law is often overwhelmed by the amount of psychological upheaval that customarily occurs when couples part. The frequent inability of couples to negotiate a successful emotional divorce has profound consequences for their children's situation and often establishes a precedent for their later dealings.

Even after they part, many couples are not at all certain that the separation is final. It has already been noted that a substantial minority of couples remain in this state of uncertainty for a long time, separating and reuniting sometimes more than once. Other couples part swiftly enough but cannot come to a custody or property settlement, facing what one team of clinicians refer to as a "divorce-transition impasse."[13] About a quarter of those who separated in the National Survey of Children had not come to a separation agreement even though they had not resided together for a year or more.

Herb and Helen, who spent about eighteen months between the separation and divorce dates, are typical of couples who divorce. Information from divorce records shows that the formal divorce process—the time between filing for a separation and receiving a divorce—takes less than two years in about 70 percent of the cases.[14] Of course, most couples are resolved to obtain a divorce by the time they make their separation official. Even so, a number of couples linger in a state of indecision before they complete divorce proceedings. And a small number of women, disproportionately black and poor, remain indefinitely separated, never reaching a final legal agreement. These women usually feel that they have nothing to gain by completing their divorces. Or they may only take final action when they anticipate remarrying, an event that rarely occurs.

In the twilight zone between marriage and divorce, when couples have not agreed to define their marriage as over, it is common to resort to makeshift and improvised arrangements regarding finances and visitation. These are frequently revised as the prospect of the divorce (or permanent separation) becomes more certain. These agreements can establish a pattern for negotiations that extends even beyond the final divorce agreement.

Herb, for example, continued to pay for the house payments and all the children's expenses after he first moved out. Still feeling that he and Helen might get back together, he never thought of cutting off payments. Besides, he was feeling very guilty about the kids. Later on, when he and Helen decided that their marriage had ended, he began to feel quite different. Helen, on the other hand, had been accustomed to receiving these payments. In the next chapter, we'll see how Herb and Helen's economic divorce actually worked out.

As in the preseparation period, enormous variation occurs in the time it takes couples to reach a more permanent child-care and property agreement. According to data from the NSC, it would appear that about half of the formerly married couples were able to work out a settlement involving finances, custody, and visitation relatively quickly, that is, within a year of the time they established separate quarters. The fact that a separation agreement is achieved quickly, however, does not necessarily imply that it is mutually acceptable or even endorsed by both parties. Fewer than a third of the respondents were able to work out an arrangement between themselves without intermediaries. In many cases, the agreement was established by third-party bargaining, was imposed by court order, or was the result of one party merely abdicating responsibility for reaching a settlement. This may explain why agreements once entered into are so frequently revised or abandoned when they prove to be unworkable. The inability to establish a firm contract early on sets the stage for disavowal and noncompliance later, when couples have presumably settled custody, property, and support arrangements.

Indeed, the very idea of a contract is inimicable to our notion of marriage. Whereas the law speaks of marriage as a contract, it is popularly construed as an emotional rather than a legal relationship. It is especially difficult, therefore, to convert a failed emotional relationship into a successful legal agreement. But although a substantial proportion of divorcing couples continue to do battle, perpetual conflict is not the norm. After the bitter recriminations preceding the separation or the painful efforts to rehabilitate the marriage, the typical pattern of most couples is to disengage physically and emotionally within a year or two of the final separation. Of course, there are the exceptions, couples who are locked in perpetual strife. But popular accounts that portray this pattern as common are wrong. By the end of the second year following separation, in all but a small minority of cases the disputes are limited to occasional flare-ups. In Spanier and Thompson's study of the process of parting, strong negative feelings among women dropped from 43 to 19 percent in the two years following separation, while for men they declined from 22 to 10 percent.[15] As time goes on, judging from NSC data, hostilities diminish further. Fewer than one in ten of the formerly married respondents who had been separated for at least five years indicated that conflict still occurred.

The transformation of relations between the formerly married partners in the year or two immediately following separation has been well documented in a series of popular and professional studies of the adjustment to divorce. Any reader of more than a few of these accounts is bound to be struck by their similarity. Robert Weiss describes the grief and longing that most couples experience as they relinquish their relationship. The writer Abigail Trafford uses the term "crazy time" to characterize the phase that couples must go through to extricate themselves from the marriage; Diane Vaughan provides a particularly astute analysis of the uncoupling process when she describes the "eradication of the marital subworld," the special set of beliefs, understandings, and sensibilities that are forged together during marriage. The obliteration of this common reality can be extremely disorienting. The process of disengagement, all agree, is generally filled with anger, grief, confusion, and depression along the way to finding emotional release and relief. One self-help book on divorce calls this time the stage of "active bleeding."[16]

THE EMOTIONAL DIVORCE

If a significant repository of trust, good will, flexibility, sympathy, and understanding remains in the marriage at the time of separation, it is often depleted in its aftermath. In extricating themselves from their marriage, individuals are laboring to establish a separate identity and an independent perspective. This inevitably involves following their own interest rather than maintaining a common interest. Kin, friends, therapists often become sympathetic allies in this pursuit.

Almost all advice books on divorce warn parents of the need to protect their children from the emotional fallout that frequently occurs as formerly married partners set about to undo the remains of their marriage. They are urged to draw a boundary around the children. Instruction such as this is offered in how to maintain the child-care system while dissolving the marital system: "It's best that you don't burden your children too much with your own worries. (Easier said than done!) Children may resent the burden or may not be able to deal with your pain (in addition to their own) . . . Be very careful about taking your anger out on your children."[17]

This advice is good but not easy to follow. Plainly, a large number of couples were unable to cooperate in childrearing before they separated. Fights over the children, complaints about parental neglect, and physical abuse within the family are common reasons why people resort to divorce. In many cases, these symptoms of family distress may be relieved but not corrected by the dissolution of the marriage. We are not suggesting that the imperatives of the emotional divorce make it impossible for parents to collaborate in childrearing. But divorce creates a classical case, in sociological parlance, of structural ambiguity. The ambiguity is that the social and psychological tasks of divorce directly collide with the normal expectations of parenthood. Most parents will have great difficulty continuing to work together in raising their children while they set about to disengage emotionally.

GENDER DIFFERENCES AND THE BREAKDOWN OF PARENTAL COOPERATION

To make matters worse, the structural fault line that jeopardizes parental collaboration in the aftermath of separation is widened by differences between men and women. Husbands and wives do not see the world alike, and their world views diverge further once their marriage ends. Jessie Bernard was among the first sociologists to observe the different perspectives in the "his and hers" marriages.[18] Men and women usually have different stakes within marriage, and their separate interests create divergent perceptions of the burdens and benefits of the marital relationship. We noted earlier in this chapter that, as a rule, women are quicker to perceive the emotional discontents in the relationship. They tend to be more sensitive to its shortfalls because they generally put more value on emotional satisfaction in marriage.

When they live together, husbands and wives trade what econo-mists call "gender-specific capital." To the extent that marriages are built upon a gender-based division of labor—and a very high pro-portion of marriages still are—husbands and wives are exchanging specialized services. In traditional marriages, he worked outside the home; she managed the domestic sphere. Of course, we know that to some degree the traditional division of labor has been altered in the last third of the twentieth century. Now both partners often work outside the home, and men share some of the domestic respon-sibilities. But in fact, most sociological research shows that the divi-sion of labor within the family has not changed as much as sometimes is imagined.[19] True, many women are working outside the home (though more often than men in part-time or irregular jobs). The evi-dence is much less clear that men are picking up the domestic slack. The husband may do a lot more than his father ever did, but if we counted who changed the most diapers or folded the most laundry, working wives would win hands down. The longstanding gender-based division of labor within the family has not disappeared despite the very substantial transformations that have taken place in the family.

When couples stop living together, the ongoing exchange between men and women seems to break down altogether. So long as they remain married, men are content to trade their higher income for the nurturing, child-care services, cooking, and housecleaning they re-ceive from their wives. When the relationship dissolves, this ex-change of benefits ceases. Accordingly, many men feel justified in withdrawing their economic support from their wives. Why, they ask, should they pay for benefits that are no longer being provided?

What's often overlooked is that men are withdrawing economic support not only from their wives but from their children as well. When Herb and Helen ended their marriage, both he and she as-sumed that the kids would stay with her. After all, she had done most of the child care while they were married. Although he wanted to continue to see his children on a regular basis, he never seriously thought of requesting physical custody. Despite the enormous changes that have occurred in our legal system over the past several decades, Herb and Helen still represent the overwhelming majority of couples. The child-care arrangements after marriage generally resemble those before the marriage ended. Women end up with most of the responsibility for the children. The custody arrangements that emerge when parents set up separate households reflect and reenforce their differing levels of involvement in child care.

Some formerly married fathers reading this book will rightly claim that they remain committed to caring for their children. They may even be assuming the lion's share of the care. With good reason, they will disassociate themselves from the generally unflattering description of divorced fathers in the discussion that follows. We acknowledge that the typical profile of the divorcing couple does not apply to all our readers. A growing number of fathers, especially among the well-educated, manage to work out some sort of shared custody arrangement or, at least, continue to play an active role in their children's upbringing. But as will become clear, these men are still exceptional. They are part of a tiny minority of all divorced fathers. A lot more behave like Herb.

CUSTODY

We are in the midst of a revolution in our custody practices, but the revolution is incomplete and its future directions unclear. Until the end of the nineteenth century, children generally lived with their fathers after a divorce occurred. Fathers maintained rights over their children, who were considered part of their property. Remember, however, that divorce was so rare that the number of children involved was small.

The routine assignment of children to their fathers began to change before the turn of the century. As men increasingly worked outside the home, the household came to be seen as women's sphere. And it was seen as the responsibility of the wife to provide nurturing and emotional support for her husband and children. Mothers were deemed more fit to care for children because of their supposedly superior moral and spiritual qualities. As a result, courts began to award custody to mothers on the grounds that children in their so-called "tender years" needed first and foremost the loving care of their mothers.[20] By the mid-twentieth century, custody was awarded to mothers in about nine out of ten cases, a proportion that has remained largely unchanged until this day.

But by the end of the 1960s, the nearly automatic preference for mother custody began to seem antiquated, even sexist—a term that didn't exist until the 1960s. Increasingly, mothers were working outside the home rather than devoting themselves solely to child care. Public opinion became more favorable to fathers' assuming a larger share of the child care, although few men actually did so. The tender-years doctrine was replaced in most states in the 1970s by the principle that custody should be awarded in the "best interests" of the child. Theoretically, this was a sex-neutral rule that allowed fathers to request custody and judges to award it to them. Yet, in practice, few fathers requested custody, and most children remained in the care of their mothers.[21]

Until the 1970s, it still was necessary for a person desiring a divorce to prove that his or her spouse had committed a grievous fault, such as abandonment, physical cruelty, or adultery. The original intent of these provisions had been to discourage couples from ending their marriages. But the presumption that one person was at fault appeared out of place in an era when most troubled marriages seemed to sink in a sea of mutual recriminations. The next wave of legal reform, which sought to eliminate the presumption of fault, began in 1969 when the California legislature enacted a statute that allowed either spouse to obtain a divorce simply on the grounds that their marriage had broken down due to irreconcilable differences. By 1985, every state allowed what came to be known as no-fault divorce.[22] But the introduction of no-fault statutes did not change custody practices much. Most children still remained in the custody of their mothers.[23]

The attempt to make the divorce process more rational also led reformers to reconsider the idea of sole custody. Many experts believed that sole custody provided legal encouragement for fathers to withdraw from child support and childrearing responsibilities. The doctrine of joint custody was promoted as a means of reducing legal battles and promoting greater paternal involvement. California was once again the pioneer when in 1979 it adopted a statute that specifically authorized joint custody and established a presumption in favor of it when it was requested by both partners; since then many other states have followed suit.

Only a few studies have examined how this recent trend toward joint custody is affecting the decisions of divorcing couples. There are two types of joint custody: joint legal custody, in which both parents share responsibility for important decisions but the children live with one parent; and joint physical custody, in which the children live for significant periods with each parent. A study of divorce cases in two northern California counties by a Stanford University research team led by Eleanor E. Maccoby and Robert H. Mnookin showed sharp changes since the introduction of the joint-custody statute. In October 1979, just 4 percent of final decrees (which were processed before the new statute went into effect) specified joint legal and physical custody and another 21 percent specified joint legal custody only. By the time 1984 and 1985 records were studied, 19 percent of new divorce petitions requested joint legal and physical custody, and an additional 39 percent requested joint legal custody only.[24]

It must be kept in mind, however, that California has been the trendsetter; joint physical custody probably is less common in other states. Census figures from 1980 show that close to 90 percent of children of formerly married parents (who were living with either parent) resided with their mothers. Infants and toddlers are about fifteen times more likely to be living with their moms. Just about 7 percent of preschoolers live with their fathers. Even among teenagers, the ratio of maternal to paternal residence is approximately seven to one. In 1980, only 13 percent of the children between ages thirteen and fifteen lived with their fathers—15 percent of the boys and 11 percent of the girls.[25]

More recent information suggests some change: from 1980 to 1986, according to the Current Population Survey, the proportion of children of formerly married parents who were in the custody of their fathers rose from 8.8 percent to 11.4 percent. Still, custodial fathers remain a rare breed. Keep in mind that even in California, according to the Stanford study, children reside with their mothers in most cases where parents have agreed to share responsibility for the children. Despite the considerable legal ferment for a more even-handed custody policy, it appears that families after divorce look very much like families before divorce. Mothers by choice or by abdication of the father are the primary if not exclusive caretakers. In Chapter 4, we will examine in more detail how children are affected by different custody arrangements.

We know rather little about how couples work out custody arrangements or even how often parents ever discuss these matters. Probably, the issue of custody never comes up in most cases. In the Stanford study, 70 percent of the couples who had received a divorce decree within three years had agreed on custody and visitation provisions with little or no conflict.[26] Like Herb and Helen, parents usually assume that existing child-care arrangements will be maintained after divorce. This does not mean that men and women are fully satisfied with the custody arrangements that evolve. Weitzman, for example, discovered that a substantial number of noncustodial fathers in her California sample claimed that they would have liked to share physical custody with their former spouses. Overall, 57 percent of fathers in her sample reported retrospectively that they wanted physical custody (compared with 98 percent of the mothers). However, about a third of these men never told their wives or mentioned it to their lawyers. And just 13 percent requested physical custody on the divorce petition. In the Stanford study, about one-third of fathers told the interviewers that they would "personally like" physical custody of their children; but more than half of these same men either did not request custody or requested mother custody on their petitions.[27]

There may be a variety of explanations for why fathers don't request physical custody more often: they may not believe that it is in the interests of their children to obtain custody; they may feel unwilling or unable to become the primary caretaker; they may regard custody as a bargaining chip for a better property settlement; or they may feel that they will not prevail in court. Weitzman concludes that most men are not seriously interested in retaining custody or, at least, have a lower stake than their former wives in the custody outcome.

We believe that the benefits of legal reform will continue to be relatively modest. As we stated earlier in this chapter, the trauma of the separation process and the need to establish an emotional divorce make it difficult for most parents to work out a viable child-care arrangement when marriages dissolve, despite custody reforms. Divorce establishes a destructive dynamic between men and women that leads many fathers to retreat from parenthood. When these men stop living with their wives and children, they no longer see themselves (or are seen by their former wives) as full-fledged fathers. It is as if their license for parenthood were revoked when their marriage ended.

FADING FATHERS

When Herb first separated, he intended to see his children regularly. Helen hoped he would. For the first year after they separated, Herb steadfastly showed up on Wednesday evenings. He would take the children out to dinner and try to catch up on the week's events, although he found these dinners frustrating. The kids couldn't remember what they had done several days before; and, for that matter, Herb didn't have much to say to them. Every other weekend the kids came to his apartment. Mickey generally slept over on Friday or Saturday, but Sally was reluctant to leave her mother overnight. These weekend visits were a little more satisfying. Herb stocked up on toys and often took the children to his parent's house, where his mother helped entertain them. Still, he recognized that being a divorced father was not at all like fatherhood used to be. Although he enjoyed playing with his children, he was not used to full-time childcare—even for a couple of days. He had relied on Helen, more than he ever thought, to make things work out with the children.

Shortly after their divorce became final, his visits became less regular. A lot of things seemed to happen at the same time: Herb became involved in a new relationship; he and Helen were having fights about money; and the kids seemed to act up all the time when he took them out. Herb told the children that he would stop the Wednesday visits if they did not behave better. His warnings were unheeded. His children seemed not to respond to his efforts to maintain a relationship with them. Herb was beginning to feel the way that many fathers do—unappreciated and rejected. These feelings made him resent all the more Helen's constant nagging at him to take more responsibility for the children. After all, they didn't seem to want to be with him. His time with them was becoming more uncomfortable and less gratifying—half the time he was angry, and half the time he felt guilty about being so angry.

After his divorce became final, Herb started to spend a lot more time with his new woman friend, Alice. Her two children were becoming fond of him, a development that Alice encouraged. Herb's warm feelings for Alice's children led him to comment to Alice: "Sometimes I think your kids care about me more than my own two children." Still, Herb managed to see his kids several times a month, and they continued to spend a week-long vacation with him at his parents' summer place.

Herb's pattern of erratic fathering is not unusual. In fact, Herb turns out to be a more conscientious father than most. Only recently did researchers begin to look at what happens to parenting practices after marriages end. They found that visiting arrangements that are worked out in the lawyer's office or the judge's chamber have little to do with what happens in reality. The discrepancy was apparent in the longitudinal study of divorcing couples in central Pennsylvania mentioned in Chapter 1. The initial interviews all were conducted within two years of the divorce. Therefore it came as a great shock that only about a third of the fathers saw their children at least once a week; and the proportion decreased further by the end of the study two and one-half years later. The results of the 1981 round of the National Survey of Children confirmed that this finding wasn't unique to central Pennsylvania. If anything, the central Pennsylvania study had overestimated the amount of paternal involvement following marital disruption. Overall, only one child in six saw his or her father as often as once a week on average. Close to half had not visited with their fathers in the 12 months preceding the survey. Another sixth had seen them less often than once a month.

Contact with nonresidential fathers dropped off sharply over time. Almost half of the children of recently separated couples saw their fathers at least once a week, and a third had not seen them at all in the past year. Among the children of marriages disrupted for ten or more years—that is, since early childhood—only one in ten had weekly contact with their fathers and almost two thirds had had no contact in the past year. Since the great majority of marriages break up while children are quite young, often in their preschool years, these findings provide an especially bleak prognosis for long-term relations between fathers and their offspring. Over time, the vast majority of children will have little or no contact with their fathers. Information from several recent surveys confirm the results of the NSC. The most recent of these studies indicates a slight rise in the proportion of fathers who have regular contact with their children. Perhaps children of divorces are seeing more of their dads. But the pattern of modest initial contact and a sharp drop-off over time is strikingly similar across studies.[28]

This pattern of visitation actually overstates the involvement of nonresidential fathers in raising their children. Even in the small number of families where children are seeing their fathers regularly, the dads assume a minimal role in the day-to-day care and supervision of their children. Children who saw their fathers at least fourteen days a year were asked how they spent time together. (It made no sense to ask this question to children who only saw their fathers on rare occasions.) Their replies indicated that most outside fathers behaved more like close relatives than parents. They took their kids on shopping trips, out to dinner, and to the movies. Sometimes they played sports with them. But routine parent–child activities were less common. Only about one child in five stated that they had carried out some project with their father, and just one in ten had been helped with their schoolwork during the preceding week. (This figure would drop to one in twenty if all children living apart from their fathers were included, regardless of whether or not they had any regular contact with their father.)

We cannot be certain, however, that fathers in intact families are much more involved with their children than nonresidential fathers. In fact, children in the NSC sample who had at least some contact with their nonresidential fathers were only slightly less likely than children from intact families to report that they frequently did things together with their fathers or that they spent as much time with them as they would like. It may be that children in intact families do not get as much attention from their fathers as they need or would like. But it is also likely that children apply a different and more generous standard when judging the actions of their noncustodial fathers. Many children appear to adopt a sliding scale for fathers who they see infrequently, stretching their standards to fit the lowered involvement. Several mothers in Terry Arendell's study of divorced families observed this pattern in their children:

> Her father takes her to lunch, maybe several times a month—if he doesn't have a girlfriend at the time. He doesn't see her that often if he has a girlfriend. She never stays over there with him, and he takes no responsibility for her. But she defends him and says he's just too busy to see her—she's doing that kind of stuff.
>
> My children adore him. He's not a very responsible human being, but they know that, and they can love him as he is.[29]

A scene from the movie *Midnight Express* also illustrates the tolerant, even indulgent, way that fathers may be viewed by their offspring. The protagonist pays an unexpected visit to his ex-wife to borrow money. Seeing his daughter for the first time in years, he immediately exchanges loving glances with her. The daughter offers her father her savings from baby-sitting jobs. The father is touched by her generosity and bids a tearful farewell, with no indication of when, if ever, he might see her again.

The deteriorating relationship between the ex-spouses is not the only reason for the decline in contact between fathers and children over time. In the next chapter, we will discuss the complex relationship between child support and visiting. Fathers who cannot or will not support their children are much more likely to stop seeing them. This means that less educated males, who have more limited employment prospects, are the most likely candidates to disappear. But plenty of middle-class men become derelict dads. A quarter of the children of college graduates in the NSC had not seen their fathers in the past year (compared with about three fifths of the children of high school dropouts).

Moreover, fathers who remarry are less likely to see their children. When fathers invest in new family responsibilities, such as having additional children, the offspring from their first marriages sometimes get short shrift. The attitude among some remarried fathers was nicely summed up by one informant in Arendell's study: "He used to have them come visit him, but he just has no room for them anymore now that he's remarried. It's like the kids don't belong in his life anymore."[30] But contact also drops off when mothers remarry. Some fathers feel rejected or displaced; others feel that the remarriage relieves them of responsibility for child care and child support. And when either parent remarries, the chance increases that he or she will move away. Study after study has demonstrated that kinship bonds are weakened by distance.[31] When a parent moves out of the home, contact with children is curtailed. But when a parent moves out of town, contact is almost always minimal. Children in the NSC were only half as likely to see their fathers weekly when they lived more than an hour away.

Surveys such as the NSC do a good job of describing statistically that most fathers, in time, withdraw from paternal responsibilities. But data from surveys do not provide a very good account of why so many men feel impelled to pull away from their children. We would argue that some men see parenting and marriage as part of the same bargain—a package deal; it is as if they stop being fathers as soon as the marriage is over. One of the women in Arendell's study said of her ex-husband: "He gets really mad if I take a particular position with the kids on anything regarding him . . . I reminded him, 'You know, you asked for these children.' He answered, 'Yes, but only as long as we were in a nuclear family.' Good grief, does that mean the children no longer exist?"[32]

Usually, however, the weakening of paternal ties occurs less abruptly and with more ambivalence—more like what happened in Herb and Helen's case. Fathers like Herb try to stay connected to their children in the early stages of marital disintegration. The problem is that it is difficult to be a part-time parent in our culture, and most fathers cannot sustain this ambiguous status very long. Americans think of parents as people who live with their children and whose business it is to know what their children are doing. Their authority arises from their role as protector and caretaker. Parents residing outside the children's home quickly become marginalized if they do not continue to play a part in the day-to-day activities of their children. Consequently, many fathers start feeling like strangers to their children, like impostors, when they see them only from time to time.

To be sure, many married men spend relatively little time in the home without losing their sense of being a father. But their wives help them maintain that identity. In intact families, mothers can do a great deal to validate the father's role in the family, particularly his relationship to his children. This is precisely what fails to occur in many disrupted families. The residential parent is frequently unwilling to support and sustain the identity of the parent living outside the children's home.

PARENTING APART

Most married parents will tell you that they have a difficult time balancing the competing demands of work and family. But it is much more difficult for parents to manage these responsibilities when they reside in separate households. The term *co-parenting*, coined by social scientists to describe the collaborative efforts of parents who live apart, implies a certain level of cooperation in the common task of childrearing. We do not have a great deal of information about the parenting practices of divorced parents. Most of what we know, however, indicates that the level of collaboration is low.

The breakdown of marital trust that occurs before and after a separation frequently disrupts a couple's ability to cooperate in childrearing. Only rarely is that ability restored with the passage of time. To be sure, most divorced parents eventually stop fighting, but they do so largely by abandoning relations altogether. A major reason why fathers stop seeing their children is that they want to have nothing to do with their former wives. And many women adopt the same attitude toward their former husbands; when they cut off contact with him, they set up barriers between him and the children. According to Wallerstein and Kelly, overburdened and angry mothers sometimes come to view the involvement of the father as nothing more than "bothersome, empty rituals." As one mother was quoted in their study, "If he didn't love you enough to stay here, then why would he visit?"[33]

These lingering resentments frequently contribute to the curtailment of fathers' involvement. To minimize the need for negotiations, fathers see their children at regular, repeated times and places, such as on certain holidays or during summer vacations. Alternatively, plans are made on an ad hoc basis by the children themselves. Herb got out of the habit of talking to Helen about the kids when they started to fight over money matters. Then when he got involved in a new relationship, he felt awkward calling Helen's house. He asked Mickey to call him and sometimes relied on his son to deliver messages to Helen. She became irritated by these instances, in her view, of irresponsible behavior. And Mickey was not always up to the task of conveying information to his mom.

A number of parents in the NSC reported that they frequently communicated through their children, presumably to avoid having to speak directly to their former spouses. So as they get older, children frequently must assume the burden themselves of working out arrangements with their nonresidential parent. Like Mickey, the children can't always handle this responsibility.

Moreover, the issue of managing parental concerns never comes up in the majority of families because the father is hardly in the picture at all. Well over half of the mothers in the NSC rarely or never talked to their former husbands about the children. Even in NSC families where regular contact between fathers and children continued, close to half of parents reported minimal or no discussions with their former partners. And even among families in the Stanford study where regular contact between fathers and children continued for three years after the separation, the most common pattern of relations was "disengaged": little cooperation, communication, or conflict.[34]

Co-parenting, then, seems to occur only in a minority of cases. The more common pattern among families in which fathers continue to see their children might be characterized as *parallel parenting*. Mothers and fathers maintain separate and segregated relations with their children and have a tacit agreement not to interfere in each other's lives. Almost never did the mothers in the NSC report that their former husbands meddled in their childrearing decisions or undermined their rules for the children—even when the fathers were quite involved in childrearing.

Parallel parenting is the best solution that many parents can work out to avoid postmarital conflict. Contact with the outside parent has the potential to aggravate old wounds or inflict new ones. So parents control conflict by maintaining separate and distinct domestic spheres. Remarriage usually reenforces the pattern of parallel parenting. As we will see in Chapter 5, new partners can occasionally play the role of intermediaries, but more often they strengthen the boundaries between households. The practice of parallel parenting has the advantage of limiting conflict in families where the non-custodial father sees the children regularly. Despite the fact that close to half of the parents in the NSC reported that they rarely or never agreed about childrearing matters, most parents reported that they rarely fought over the children. What's more, their children seemed to concur with this assessment. Only one in seven children in the NSC stated that their parents sometimes or often fought over them.

This style of conflict management, however, has some drawbacks for children. They are forced to maintain a highly segregated existence in their divided families. They are often called upon not to report what happened when they were at Mom or Dad's house. And they frequently are exposed to conflicting rules and standards. No one really knows, however, whether this sort of bicultural family existence is harmful to children or, for that matter, whether children do a lot better when their parents remain in close contact. There are also some disadvantages for parents who opt for parallel parenting. They are probably more likely to misperceive, misreport, and misinterpret the motives and actions of each other when communication is so limited. Custodial mothers may feel that their former husbands' reluctance to communicate causes them to take too little responsibility in raising the children. And fathers, in contrast, may believe that their former wives, by refusing to communicate, have shut them out of important decisions affecting their children's lives.

CO-PARENTING VS. PARALLEL PARENTING

Some parents nevertheless are able to share parenting responsibilities quite well after divorce. The kids and their teddy bears shuttle back and forth between two households. Their parents discuss arrangements civilly, if not amicably. They show up together at PTA meetings, sit next to each other at soccer games, and chat comfortably at graduation ceremonies. We know some families like these, and the reader may, too. But it is hazardous to generalize from personal impressions. These families are somewhat more prevalent among the middle-class and much more common in academic and professional circles. They are the ones that stand out in our minds and that journalists love to write about. Even so, we would wager that if most readers made a full list of all the divorced persons that they know with children, they would discover that relatively few fit this collaborative model.

An estimate of the prevalence of co-parenting can be obtained from the 1981 NSC, using the reports of custodial mothers in families in which fathers saw their children at least once a week. In that small subset, we relied on the custodial mother's report of how much she and the child's father consulted with one another, avoided fighting too much, and shared the decision making. Under this standard, only 25 percent of the subset maintained collaborative relations. Of course, virtually none of the many more families with irregular or no contact were co-parenting. If we include all families, consequently, the proportion of collaborative parents declines to just 9 percent.

These estimates probably are low. Since 1981, the movement toward joint custody, the greater involvement of fathers in childrearing, and the normalization of divorce may have all contributed to increasing the incidence of postmarital collaboration between parents. Moreover, the NSC figures are based on children who were eleven to sixteen, whose parents may be less likely to communicate than are those with younger children.

More recent estimates from the Stanford study, based on interviews between 1985 and 1989, are somewhat higher. About one and a half years after the separation, children in two thirds of the families were seeing their nonresident parent at least once every two weeks. And among this subset, 26 percent of parents were said to have "cooperative" relations—they talked frequently, coordinated rules, backed each other up, managed the logistics of visiting, and didn't argue much. So among all families, including those in which the children didn't see their nonresident parent regularly, about one out of six—still a distinct minority—had a cooperative pattern.[35] When the Stanford study again interviewed the families about three and a half years after the separation, they found that the proportion of families with a cooperative style was quite similar. But there had been a large increase—from 29 to 41 percent—in the number of parents that were "disengaged," characterized by low communication and low conflict. A minority could cooperate well; those who could not had increasingly withdrawn from each others' lives.[36]

To be sure, the ranks of cooperative parents may continue to increase as custody practices encourage joint responsibility. Nonetheless, we doubt that cooperative parenting will ever become the typical pattern following marital disruption. And we especially question whether joint physical custody will ever become much more prevalent than it is today. Parents who cannot get along when they are married are unlikely to work out their differences when they are divorced. Remarriage usually widens the emotional gulf between the formerly married couple, further reducing the prospects for close collaboration. Enthusiasm about the benefits of joint physical custody for children may have peaked. Some early proponents of joint physical custody have begun to express doubts that it should be the preferred standard.[37] It often encourages couples to enter an agreement that may be unworkable, especially if one parent has a limited commitment to childrearing or if they cannot cooperate. The sad fact is that many parents are incapable of putting their marital conflicts behind them. For those who are determined to preserve their enmity—or who cannot avoid doing so—joint physical custody may be the worst possible arrangement for their children.

Is our account of the barriers to achieving parental cooperation too pessimistic? Many have argued that parents can be assisted in managing the divorce transition better.[38] Marital therapy, divorce mediation, family counseling, and self-help groups have expanded in recent decades to assist parents in working out relations after divorce. Indeed, parents going through the process of divorce face a bewildering set of helpers. Perhaps Herb could have been helped to see more clearly how he was contributing to his children's adjustment problems. Had he been aided in dealing with his confusion, his self-doubt, and his guilt at the time of the divorce, then he might not have been so injured by his children's understandable reserve. Perhaps he then might have been induced to maintain more active ties with them in the year or two following his divorce.

We think it is likely that many parents, like Herb, could benefit from counseling, mediation, and other forms of therapy during the early stages of divorce. But we doubt that most participants in counseling programs develop a lasting capacity to cooperate closely with their former spouses. It is more realistic to believe that these couples could be coaxed into adopting the style of childrearing that we called parallel parenting—low conflict with a modest amount of consultation. That may be as much as we can hope for, given the deep-seated reasons that formerly married couples have for not cooperating.

Herb, for example, was not well prepared for childcare; Helen had done most of the parenting up to the time of the divorce. Then, too, his family situation was complicated by his relationship with Alice and her kids. It remains an open question whether counseling could have affected the long-term course of Herb's paternal involvement.

But counselors and mediators may perform an important social function apart from their success in altering the behavior of their particular clients. At a social and cultural level, these programs promulgate the idea that parents can and should cooperate in their children's best interests. In setting a higher standard than most parents actually attain, the helping professions fashion expectations for all parents—the participants and the nonparticipants alike—that cooperation is desirable and is possible.

It is unavoidable that this new normative standard will clash with the difficult reality of parenting apart. With resources, dedication, and social support, a small but perhaps growing minority of parents will manage to work together in raising their children. A larger number will establish a pattern of parallel parenting, conducting their parenting roles as separately as possible. But in many other cases—approaching a majority—the nonresidential parent will abdicate virtually all responsibility. It is in these families that children may be most at risk—at least economically. The next chapter looks at the economic fortunes of mothers and children when fathers disappear.

CHAPTER 3

The Economic Consequences of Divorce

Academics and clinicians debate how much divorce affects the per-sonality, values, and behavior of children. But the economic effects are hardly ever disputed. Divorce often results in a sharp drop in the standard of living of children and their custodial parents. It carries many families into poverty and locks others into economic disadvantage for lengthy spells.

Here are the bleak facts. In 1988, 16 percent of all families with children under age 18 were poor—by itself, a shocking figure. But among female-headed families with children under 18, 45 percent were poor. In contrast, 7 percent of families with children headed by a married couple were living in poverty. In other words, families with children are more than six times as likely to be poor if they are headed by a mother alone than if they are headed by two parents.[1] Researchers who have followed families over time have found that these spells of poverty often begin just after the disruption of a marriage. According to one study, about 10 percent of white children and 14 percent of black children whose parents separated fell into poverty the following year.[2] Moreover, the study showed that families with a single parent were much less likely to escape from poverty. Overall, white children growing up in single-parent families spent an average of 3.2 years in poverty during their childhood, whereas those who lived continuously in two-parent families spent just 0.5 years in poverty.[3]

This chapter explains why a lowered standard of living is a likely

46   consequence of marital dissolution for children. In exploring the reasons why, we inevitably confront one of the most pressing policy issues of our day: what, if anything, can be done to break the link between family change and economic disadvantage? Although a full treatment of the policy alternatives will be reserved for the final chapter, the evidence suggests that our peculiarly American view of marital and family responsibilities is strongly implicated in the economic plight of children. In America we leave it up to individual couples to sort out their personal affairs when their marriages break up. The state only becomes an active party when they cannot resolve their differences. But this strong commitment to letting divorcing couples reach their own private agreements often works to the disadvantage of mothers and children.

HOW THE SYSTEM WORKS

Just as there are no guidelines for couples on how to accomplish an emotional divorce, there are no guidelines for working out an economic settlement either. In fact, getting an economic divorce raises many of the same issues that couples face in sorting out marital and childrearing responsibilities. Once again, the gender-based division of labor in the family is at the heart of the problem. The family has always functioned as an economic distribution system, channeling resources from productive members to dependents such as children and the elderly. During the early years of industrialization, many older children worked for wages which they contributed to the family. Most wives contributed largely through household tasks, childrearing, or taking in boarders and lodgers. Then, in the early part of this century, children's earnings became less central to the household economy, and men, to a growing extent, became the primary wage earners. More recently, working wives have shared this role, although their earnings rarely equal their husbands'.[4]

The fact that men and women contribute unequal amounts to the total family income poses no problem so long as the family continues to operate as a common unit. Men and women trade labor inside and outside the home to the benefit of all family members. But divorce disrupts the family distribution system. Most fathers still rely on their former wives to care for the children, and most mothers still expect financial support from their former husbands—even though they don't live together. Dependent children must be guaranteed domestic stability and economic security even though parents no longer pool resources. Unfortunately, there is no formula for converting a two-parent household economy into two separate units.

Lacking such a formula, it is up to the conflicting parties to arrive at a fair settlement for dividing economic assets and obligations. And if the husband and wife are unable to agree, they have recourse to the legal system. In this sense, they bargain, as two legal scholars have put it, in the "shadow of the law."[5] These private negotiations are supposed to lead to an equitable economic settlement which also protects the children's interests. Unfortunately, the evidence suggests otherwise. Generally, what happens is that the economic pie is sliced into unequal parts, and men are served a larger helping at the expense of the rest of the family.

A good way to illustrate the problem is to see how Herb and Helen managed their economic divorce. At the time of their separation, Herb was the assistant manager of a fast-food franchise. He was earning about $24,000 per year. Helen had recently returned to work as a part-time secretary. She made $8,000 in the year before the marriage broke up. They had moved into a $60,000 condominium garden apartment only a year before the separation occurred. Although both Herb's and Helen's parents had helped them make the down payment, the furnishings and monthly payments had depleted their modest savings, leaving almost no cash reserves at the time of their separation.

The custody of the children was never an issue between them. Herb was deeply attached to his five-year-old son but assumed that the kids would stay with Helen. Her concern for the children led Herb to make what he thought was a generous settlement. He gave up his modest equity—about $10,000—in the condominium and took only a few of the furnishings for his small apartment. He got to keep the car, which permitted him to visit the children. In return, Helen agreed not to request any alimony and to accept a monthly child-support payment of $300, 15 percent of Herb's gross income.

Herb and Helen soon faced the harsh economic realities of divorce. It is far more expensive to maintain separate households. Even though Helen began to work full time, her financial situation worsened. She was now fully responsible for the mortgage and for the remaining payments on the furnishings. In addition her child-care costs doubled. She had counseling bills for her son, who was having trouble at school; and she badly needed a car to manage her complicated work and child-care schedule. She was starting to have trouble meeting the monthly payments. A move to a smaller place would have been less expensive, but she would have saved only about $100 a month and would have had to move out of the neighborhood, which was within walking distance of her parents' home.

Helen soon asked Herb to increase his monthly payments, but he resisted. After meeting his apartment expenses, the car payments, and his child support, he had little discretionary income. Some months after his final separation Herb started dating Alice, whose husband had stopped paying child support a few years after he moved in with a new partner. Herb realized that if he and his new partner got serious, he would have to cut down on the monthly payments to Helen in order to help support this new household. Naturally, he had not yet broached the subject of reducing the monthly payments with Helen, who was still complaining about living on her tight budget.

Herb and Helen epitomize the normal American way of reallocating economic responsibilities following divorce. If anything, they managed the situation more equitably than do most couples. But it does not take an accountant to recognize that in the postmarital bargaining, Helen and the two kids lost out economically when Herb moved out. She assumed full responsibility for supporting the children on a family income of $17,600 ($14,000 salary plus $3,600 in child support). Herb may feel disadvantaged relative to his standard of living before the separation, but in fact he is making out pretty well. Herb has discharged his economic responsibilities by providing $3,600 a year, retaining $20,400 for his own support.

When marriages dissolve, the shift in family responsibilities and family resources assumes a characteristic form. Women get the children and, accordingly, assume most of the economic responsibility for their support. Men become nonresidential parents and relinquish the principal responsibility for their children's support. Men, like Herb, may believe that they are making economic sacrifices equivalent to their former wives. But the facts don't generally support their contention.

ECONOMIC STATUS BEFORE AND AFTER DIVORCE

Herb and Helen are by no means among the most disadvantaged of divorcing couples. And Helen, despite her very real economic troubles, is undoubtedly better off than many divorcing women. Together, she and Herb were earning close to the median family income, and they had some property to divide. Forty percent of all couples who divorce make no property settlement because there is nothing of value to divide.[6] (If we were to add to that figure the couples who separate but never divorce, the proportion of those without property would be even higher.)

In addition, Herb agreed to let Helen keep the condominium for the sake of the children, foregoing his share of the equity. Had he not done so, Helen would have been forced to sell the property immediately. Most divorcing couples with some tangible assets are in Herb and Helen's situation. Their home is the only item of real value. So in order to divide the property evenly, it is often necessary to sell the house. In Lenore Weitzman's study of divorce settlements in California, about a third of court-ordered divorces required the sale of the family home.[7] Other studies indicate the situation in California is not unique. The proportion of couples that liquidate the family home after divorce seems to be rising.[8] The loss of the family home is one of the most disruptive consequences of divorce. As we shall soon see, moving away from a familiar environment often starts a chain of social transitions resulting in profound, and sometimes damaging, psychological changes.

Furthermore, Herb is dutifully paying close to 15 percent of his annual income in child support. Not nearly enough, you may be saying, but Herb's perception from talking to the guys is that he is paying more than most. He is correct. The government publishes figures on the amount of child support that women with children under 21 receive from fathers living outside the children's home.[9] Among women who had been married (as opposed to those who had given birth out of wedlock), about one fourth had no child-support agreement in 1987. And among those who had an agreement, one fourth reported that no support payments were made in that year. Thus, roughly two fifths of all previously married fathers contributed nothing at all to their children's support. Among the other three fifths, the amount of child support paid averaged about $235 a month. Child-support payments amount to only about 10 percent of the income of separated and single mothers and 13 percent of the income of divorced mothers. By this standard, Herb's modest contribution of $3,600, which amounts to 20 percent of Helen's income, is relatively generous.

In noting that Herb is paying more than most men, we are not implying that he is paying a fair share. Helen and her two children clearly are not making out very well, and his limited contribution is part of the reason. The cost of raising a preschool child in 1985 at a modest standard of living was about $4,500 a year, excluding child-care expenses.[10] It is difficult to estimate the additional cost of a second child, but let's assume it is about 50 percent of the cost of the first. At best, then, Herb is only covering about two fifths of his children's real expenses—and much less if child care is included. Furthermore, the costs of raising children rise as they get older. But Herb's agreement with Helen, like most, makes no allowance for their changing needs or even for inflation. Consequently, although Herb is making more than half again as much as Helen, he is paying far less than she is for their children's support, and the level of support he is providing will undoubtedly shrink in purchasing power over time.

According to one national study that followed families throughout the 1970s, women suffer about a 30 percent decline, on average in their income in the year following a separation, whereas men experience a 15 percent increase.[11] The divergence can be explained partly by men's greater earning capacity. On average women earn only about two thirds of what men earn. As long as families pool their incomes, this disparity is of no special economic consequence to women and children. But when marriages dissolve, women must support themselves and their children with their lower incomes and with child-support payments, if any, from their former husbands. It is debatable whether divorce ought to change the relative economic standing of men and women. Some economists would argue that women who seek divorce are trading off a better standard of living for improved psychological well-being. But this reasoning takes no account of the children.

How much difference would it make to children if ex-husbands like Herb paid a fairer share? It is not easy to arrive at a precise formula, but one widely accepted standard was devised by Irwin Garfinkel, a leading authority on child support.[12] Taking into account both children's needs and the capacity of an absent parent to pay, Garfinkel developed a scheme that is now being applied in Wisconsin; variations on it have been adopted by about half of the other states. Noncustodial fathers are required to pay a fixed proportion of their gross income that varies according to the number of children they have, ranging in Wisconsin from 17 percent per year for one child to 34 percent per year for five or more.

Garfinkel's standard would greatly alter the agreement Helen and Herb reached on their own. Instead of paying $3,600, Herb would have to contribute $6,000—an increase of two thirds. Their standard of living would be more equal: Herb would end up with a gross income of $18,000 and Helen and her children would have $20,000. In families of modest means, like Herb and Helen's, raising the level of child support to a fairer standard makes a dramatic difference in the family income of a female household head and her children. If implemented nationwide, the Garfinkel formula would increase the total amount of child support due by about 69 percent—just by applying a common standard. And if money were collected from all absent fathers, the current level of child support provided to women would be tripled.[13] At 1985 levels, the average amount of child support would rise to more than $6,500. This figure, however, assumes perfect compliance, which no one thinks is possible. Toward the end of this chapter and in Chapter 6, we will consider the problems of collecting child support and some of the proposed solutions for increasing compliance.

Some skeptical observers have questioned how well this policy of redistributing resources from men to women and children will actually work. It is based on the assumption that most males can afford to pay a larger share of their earnings than they do now. At higher income levels, especially for formerly married fathers, such an assumption may be warranted. Even for men of more modest means, like Herb, there is probably substantial room for redistribution. But at lower income levels, it may not be so easy or profitable to collect from formerly married men, not to mention never married fathers. Thus, we should not hold out high hopes that a better system of child support will solve the problem of poverty arising from marital dissolution among low-income families. Estimates indicate a modest reduction in poverty can be achieved, and it will be most evident for white women and their children, whose ex-husbands are better able to pay adequate support levels. Among black men, who more often have limited earning capacities, increasing child-support payments will be difficult to accomplish and may do little more than rearrange which families are poor.[14]

WHAT ECONOMIC DECLINE MEANS TO CHILDREN

Even if elevating the level of child support would not solve all economic problems, it would be likely to diminish the extreme poverty of some female-headed families and to cushion the economic fall of many others. The national data show that currently divorced women and their children do not regain their predivorce standard of living until five years after the breakup, on average.[15] And these aggregate figures conceal sharp differences according to women's circumstances. Women who were married to men with high earnings typically experience a sharper decline in living standard than women who were already poor, and they recover more slowly. Like Helen, most women cannot immediately regain their economic losses by working more. If they have been out of the job market or only working part time, it takes a long while before they acquire skills and experience needed to earn enough to support a family. One study shows that, in time, many improve their situation by career advancement.[16] In the short term, though, the surest means to a quick economic recovery is through remarriage. This is one of the main reasons why black women—who generally have poorer prospects for remarriage—are less likely than whites to recover economically from a divorce.

So a woman's economic position remains tied to her marital status even after she divorces. Many separated and divorced women will remain near or below the poverty line for several years unless they remarry. What this means for women and children is that every year a million families experience a drop in income that is similar to what families went through during the Great Depression.[17] This income loss is usually accompanied by a host of related life changes. To see this more clearly, let's return to our case history and watch what happened to Helen and her children after her divorce became final.

Remember that Helen was wondering whether she could afford to meet the payments on her new condominium. After six months of falling further and further behind, she decided that she had to sell it. She and the children temporarily took refuge with her parents while she paid off some of her debts. This gave her time to look around for suitable housing, but it was difficult for her son Mickey, who did not want to move away from the kids on his block. Unfortunately, the move also required that the children switch schools. Mickey, who had experienced some difficulties in kindergarten before the move, began to have academic problems in the first grade, which were aggravated by the adjustment to a new school. The teacher advised Helen to have Mickey repeat the first grade.

Helen's parents were supportive and helpful, but she did not feel comfortable staying with them indefinitely. Her younger brother was still at home, and he often woke the kids up when he came in late. Sally was sharing a room with Helen, an arrangement that would not work indefinitely. Helen did not want to put the two children in the same room. So she found an apartment near her work. It was in a less desirable section of the city, farther away from her parents, but it provided the necessary space at an affordable price.

A few weeks before Helen and her kids moved into the apartment, Herb told Helen that he could not afford to keep up the payments at the existing level. He had begun living with Alice, the woman he had been dating, and her two children. Already anticipating marriage, he expected to help support his new family. Herb's visits with Mickey and Sally were becoming more irregular. Although still attached to his son, Herb sometimes felt that Mickey was a stranger to him. And he felt as though he hardly knew his daughter. Herb began to ask himself why he should pay for kids whom he seldom saw. He was rapidly becoming more attached to Alice's children, feeling that they were just as much his responsibility as his own children. Besides, Helen was working full time. She had cleared some money from the condominium sale and was now living in less expensive housing.

Herb's threats to reduce his support payments and his decreased contact with the kids were making Helen feel desperate. She was furious about Herb's relationship with Alice, and her rage sometimes spilled over to Mickey, especially when he wanted to talk about his visits with his dad and Alice and her family. Helen did not know whether to see a therapist or a lawyer. In the second year after her divorce, she ended up seeing both, further draining her limited economic reserves. Even with her lower rent, Helen was barely making it; so she reluctantly accepted overtime work at the office to help meet the expenses. This gave her even less time with the children, whom she knew needed more of her attention.

Helen's experiences are typical of many women in the aftermath of a divorce.[18] So, too, are her children's experiences. Katherine Newman describes the economic trajectory of most divorced women as a process of "falling from grace."[19] Helen, like many others after divorce, fell from the middle-class and took her children with her. She moved twice in less than two years, trading home ownership for cheaper housing in a less desirable neighborhood. She increased her working hours and decreased the time she was able to spend with her children.

Sara McLanahan, in a study of the economic consequences of divorce, discovered that almost two fifths of divorced mothers move in the first year after divorce, a rate far higher than the occurence for stably married families during the same interval.[20] Even after the first year, divorced women continue to move at a rate of about 20 percent a year, about one third more often than women in intact marriages. More of the moves reported by divorced women resulted from necessity than choice, especially in the immediate aftermath of divorce. During the first year after divorce, 15 percent of the divorced women were forced to move—seven times the rate of forced moves among stably married women.

Many women, like Helen, take temporary shelter in their parents' households. About 7 percent of formerly married women with children were living with their parents at the time of the 1980 census. Moreover, this snapshot picture greatly underestimates the proportion who ever move back home after a divorce. Among separated and divorced women with younger children—who are probably nearer to the time of the separation—17 percent were living with their parents in 1980.[21] Doubling up has some economic and psychological benefits for divorced mothers and their children. However, it is not generally the preferred arrangement of most divorced women or even of their parents, who often find the arrangement stressful. One study reported a sharp rise in family conflict after members began sharing a household.[22] A national study of grandparents revealed that parents frequently provided substantial assistance to recently divorced women and their children but that intergenerational relations sometimes became intrusive. Divorced women complained that grandparents all too frequently interfered with their parental authority or intruded in their family affairs.[23] And another investigation concluded that heavy reliance on parents sometimes hinders a divorced mother's ability to adjust to her new status.[24]

Many women also share Helen's experience of longer hours at work and less time at home. One study found that the proportion of women working 1,000 hours a year or more rose from 51 to 73 percent after a separation, and their incomes increased proportionately.[25] Women who remain unmarried are especially likely to increase their working hours, often taking new jobs in order to do so. Another study discovered higher rates of both quitting and being laid off in the year after divorce.[26]

These residential and occupational changes are part of a familiar pattern that divorced women exhibit. As Helen's case illustrates, economic and emotional losses are often confounded. Even among women who welcomed the dissolution of their marriages, the confluence of events that accompany a sharp drop in income and living standard is bound to create great stress. And this stress often reverberates in ways that affect the children. Helen had less time to spend with Mickey and Sally. They were subjected to several unexpected and unwanted moves. For Mickey, the timing was especially unfortunate, for it exacerbated his school problems. Helen's anger over Herb's economic threats (and his new relationship) complicated her dealings with her son. In ways such as these, the children of divorce are both directly and indirectly affected by a sudden economic drop. In this respect, they share many of the emotional problems experienced by the children who went through the Great Depression.[27]

We are happy to report that things eventually settled down for Helen and her children. Herb backed down from his threat to reduce child support when he was notified by Helen's lawyer that he would face court action. In addition, Herb realized that he was not making out badly at all. The child-support payments had not gone up in the two years since his divorce, whereas his salary had risen to $28,500, an increase of nearly 20 percent. Herb's change in attitude improved his relationship with Helen. His visits with the children, however, were becoming even more irregular since Helen stopped prodding him to see them.

For her part, Helen learned to make do with less. She made friends in the apartment building and joined a baby-sitting co-op. But Mickey still is not doing well in school. The second move created more academic problems, but at least he is getting along better with his schoolmates. Helen is feeling less depressed and is managing her life much better. She is calmer with the kids and has learned from her therapy just to listen sympathetically to Mickey when he talks about his dad. But despite Helen's recovery, she and her children are not living as well—materially at least—as they were three years earlier. Moreover, they are not nearly as well off as Herb and his new family. Herb is combining his income of $28,500 (effectively $24,900 when child-support payments are deducted) with Alice's earnings of $15,000. Together, their family income of $43,500 places them both in a higher income bracket than either was in during their first marriages. Compared with Helen, Mickey, and Sally, Herb has little to complain about. In contrast, Herb's former wife and children have been subjected to a series of stressful events partly or wholly because they became poorer.

WHY DON'T FATHERS PAY MORE?

Government statistics on alimony and child support were not compiled before the early 1970s. Between 1970 and 1978, no significant changes occurred. For example, only 10 percent of women actually received alimony in 1978 (of the 14.3 percent women awarded alimony, 70 percent collected some payments). By 1985 this figure had risen ever so slightly to 10.7 percent (73 percent of the 14.6 percent awarded alimony). Weitzman marshals some evidence to show that recent divorce settlements provide less well for women than those occurring a decade or more ago. But her argument holds, at best, for middle-class women leaving long-standing marriages. This group is probably significantly worse off today than they were in the past. We doubt that other formerly married women were better off a few decades ago; rather, we think they were not provided for then and they are still not provided for today.

We suspect that most men, divorced fathers included, strongly adhere to the belief that fathers should be obliged to pay their fair share of their children's support.[28] If this is true, how can we then account for the seemingly callous behavior of many males? One reason, mentioned earlier, is that some men do not have the money to provide much assistance. Unemployed, underemployed, and low-wage-earning fathers may have little to share with their children. Yet this explanation hardly seems sufficient to explain why two fifths of all formerly married fathers pay nothing at all. Evidence from a variety of sources indicates that almost all formerly married fathers could pay something, and most are capable of paying far more than they do.[29] And men who may not be able to pay much at the time of divorce often improve their economic circumstances in time.

The Census Bureau conducted a survey on child support in 1987 in which women without a child-support agreement were asked why they had failed to get one.[30] A small proportion had settled for a property settlement instead of child support. The rest were evenly divided between women who said they had not asked for child support and those who had asked for child support but could not

58   obtain an award. Why should any mother with children not insist on a child-support award? There is no single answer to this question. Some divorcing women refuse a settlement as a way of distancing themselves from their former spouses. Some bargain away child support for exclusive custody rights. In their view, it is not worth a few thousand dollars to have to deal with their former spouse or to have him involved with their children. Women who have remarried or reentered relationships may be especially inclined to dismiss their former spouses from economic obligations. Many women, one study reports, came to expect so little economic support from their ex-husbands while they were married that they were relieved at not having him "take money out of the till."[31]

For one reason or another, then, a substantial number of women are willing to pay, in effect, to stop their former husbands from interfering in their affairs. Many more women, however, would like to collect support but are unable to get a binding agreement. Some fathers simply disappear when the marriage ends—they don't stay around long enough to negotiate a settlement. In the Census Bureau survey, the most common reason that women report for why they were not able to reach a child-support agreement was that they were unable to locate the father. And even when fathers remain in the picture, it is often difficult to get them to pay. In Terry Arendell's study of middle-class divorced mothers, several women told her that they had given up on trying to obtain child support because they lacked the resources, energy, or persistence to obtain a binding agreement. Arendell concludes that women often are intimidated by the legal system, which appears to them as unresponsive, if not unsympathetic, to their children's needs.[32]

Her conclusions echo a theme sounded by others who have examined how the judicial system functions. Weitzman argues that, in child-support disputes, the courts are biased in favor of fathers. In response to a series of hypothetical cases, American judges were much less sensitive to children's economic needs and more sensitive to men's economic needs than their British counterparts. She concludes that our system seems to put "fathers first," ahead of mothers and their children. We agree that the legal system must receive some of the blame for the low levels of child support in this country.[33]

But there are other, more subtle, factors at work that are linked to gender differences in the way that men and women deal with economic matters. Researchers such as Weitzman and Arendell point out that men (and their attorneys) are more likely than women to view the care and custody of children as part of the settlement package which includes property and child support. Women, on the other hand, usually view custody as a separate issue of the highest importance. Therefore, in order to retain custody, women tend to compromise more easily on the economic matters.[34]

Many of the same factors that prevent women from obtaining a child-support award in the first place also prevent them from enforcing awards that are in effect. In 1985, over 75 percent of divorced women received child-support awards, but only three quarters of these women were collecting any payments. Just about half received the full amount of support due. Consistent with the pattern of visitation described in the previous chapter, support payments generally dwindle as time goes on. Just as Herb was tempted to do, many men fail to make good on their original agreement—even though most child-support payments shrink in purchasing power because they are not adjusted for cost of living. And again, the legal system is often not much help:

> We've got a court order for child support. Last year, when I knew my ex-husband had a job and where, I tried to go through my attorney to get enforcement. But all that happened was that I got stuck with court costs and attorney's fees, and I didn't get any money in return. I did have a lien on his paycheck once. I got like two hundred dollars that way, and he promptly got fired. That's the only thing I ever got from him. It just didn't pay off.[35]

There are many reasons, including economic ones, why men fail to pay the amount agreed upon. Remarriage by either partner often erodes a man's commitment to child support. When they remarry, men like Herb often feel entitled to reduce their support payments because they have a second family to support. When custodial mothers remarry, fathers frequently see this as an opportunity for reducing support payments, reasoning that their economic assistance is needed less.[36] Father's rights groups contend that many men fail to live up to their support agreements because their former wives deny them access to their children. But as far as we can tell, fathers who must resort to economic retaliation because they are locked out of their children's homes are a tiny minority. These incidents tend to receive more attention than the much more common instances of families in which men withdraw economic support before or concurrently with their diminished involvement with their children.[37]

The weight of the admittedly incomplete evidence suggests to us that most men pay little or no child support because they can get away with it. The gender-based division of labor in the family leads many men to see their children as women's responsibility. In the abstract, most men will say that a father's obligation to his children is inviolable. In practice, many fathers cut lose from their children soon after their marriages end.

Yet just as often, men find themselves in Herb's situation. They begin their postdivorce lives with a strong commitment to support their children. Over time, their resolution weakens as relations with their children become emotionally less rewarding or they acquire a new set of family commitments. In effect these men trade in old obligations for new ones. From their point of view, they are not callously disregarding their family responsibilities but rather redefining them as they move from one marriage to the next. This pattern points to an unresolved policy issue. How do we reconcile the economic obligations of parents to their different sets of offspring and to their biological and sociological dependents? In contrast with many other Western nations, the United States has until recently favored a voluntary approach to child support. In effect, fathers have been allowed to put their money where their heart is. And many fathers have opted to invest most if not all of their resources in their current household rather than their former one. If all women reentered marriage soon after divorce, this arrangement would work well enough. But fewer women than men remarry, and our society has begun to realize the high costs to children of letting fathers decide whether their first loyalties are to their present or past families.

WHERE DO WE GO FROM HERE?

To the extent that fathers retain an emotional stake in their children, we think this will increase their sense of economic obligation. But the process of cultural change in the role of fathers is likely to be gradual. In the meantime, we must look to other means of securing economic support from fathers.

Concern about the meager level of child support and about the dependency of many female-headed families on public assistance led to the passage of Federal child-support legislation in 1984 and 1988. These laws mandate state guidelines for minimum support levels and better mechanisms, including wage garnishing, for collecting support payments. A decade earlier, such measures would have been unimaginable in the United States. Evidently, we are slowly abandoning our voluntary, do-it-yourself approach to child support. It remains to be seen whether this nationalized approach to child-support collection will work as well in the United States as it appears to in some European nations. In the final chapter, we will examine these new policies and their prospects for success.

During the 1980s, we witnessed a growing wave of interest in fatherhood. Indeed, if one takes seriously the popular and professional outpouring of materials, it would be only a slight exaggeration to conclude that American males are currently in the midst of a cult of fatherhood. More fathers are participating in the delivery process, taking time off from work to care for their children, and sharing more of the care of their preschoolers. Yet it is hard to determine just how many men have been enlisted in this movement; we suspect that there is still more talk than action. Nonetheless, the trend toward greater involvement of fathers is real and could have consequences for fathers' behavior after divorce. As commitment to fatherhood rises, a shrinking fraction of men will sever the bonds with their children simply because they no longer reside with them.

CHAPTER 4

Children's Adjustment
to Divorce

As Helen watched, Sally, then three, walked over to where her six-year-old brother was playing and picked up one of his toy robots. Mickey grabbed the robot out of her hand, shouted "No!" and pushed her away. The little girl fell backward and began to cry. Helen had just finished another frustrating phone call with Herb, who had told her that he could no longer afford to pay as much child support as they had agreed. She was grateful to her parents for allowing her and the kids to live with them temporarily, but the crowded household was beginning to strain everyone's patience. She rushed over to her daughter, picked her up, and shouted at her son, "Don't you hit her like that!" "But it was mine," he said, whereupon he took another robot and threw it on the floor near his mother's feet. She grabbed his arm and dragged him to his room, screaming at him all the way.

Then she sat down in the living room, with Sally in her lap, and reflected on how often scenes such as this were occurring. Ever since the separation eight months earlier, she had had a hard time controlling Mickey. He disobeyed her, was mean to his sister, and fought with friends in school. And when he talked back to her, she lost her temper. But that just made him behave worse, which in turn made her angrier, until he was sent to his room and she sat down, distraught.

Helen's problems with her son fit a pattern familiar to psychologists who study the effects of divorce on children, an escalating cycle of misbehavior and harsh response between mothers and sons. But not all parents and children become caught up in these so-called coercive cycles after the breakup of a marriage. Studies show a wide range of responses to divorce. Some children do very well; others fare poorly. In this chapter we will examine these differences and inquire into why they occur.

We tend to think of divorce as an event that starts when a husband or wife moves out of their home. But it is often more useful to think of divorce as a process that unfolds slowly over time, beginning well before the separation actually occurs. In many cases it is preceded by a lengthy period of conflict between the spouses. It is reasonable to expect that this predisruption conflict, and the corresponding emotional upset on the part of the parents, may cause problems for children.

For example, when things began to heat up between Mickey and his mother, Helen naturally assumed that the problems between them were largely the result of the divorce. Perhaps she was right. But her guilty feelings made Helen conveniently forget that Mickey had had behavioral problems for several years—ever since the quarreling between his parents became severe. Almost two years before the separation, Mickey's preschool teacher had asked Helen if things were going all right at home. Mickey had displayed unusual fits of temper with his classmates and seemed distracted during play periods. If you had asked Mickey's teacher, she would have predicted that Mickey, although bright enough, was going to have adjustment problems in kindergarten. And so he did. True, Mickey's problems did get worse the year that his parents separated, but it is not obvious that his difficulties in school would have been avoided even if his parents had managed to remain together.

In fact, there is evidence that some children show signs of disturbance months, and sometimes even years, before their parents separate. In 1968 a team of psychologists began to study three-year-olds at two nursery schools in Berkeley, California. The psychologists followed these children and their families, conducting detailed personality assessments at ages four, five, seven, eleven, and fourteen. When the study started, 88 children were living with two married parents. Twenty-nine of these children experienced the breakup of their parents' marriages by the time they were fourteen. Curious as to what the children were like before the breakup, the psychologists paged backward through their files until they found the descriptions of the children eleven years earlier, when they were age three.

The results were quite dramatic for boys. Years before the breakup, three-year-old boys whose families eventually would disrupt were more likely to have been described as having behavioral problems than were three-year-old boys whose families would remain intact. According to the researchers, Jeanne H. Block, Jack Block, and Per F. Gjerde, three-year-old boys who would eventually experience family disruption already were rated as more "inconsiderate of other children, disorderly in dress and behavior," and "impulsive," and more likely to "take advantage of other children." Moreover, their fathers were more likely to characterize themselves as often angry with their sons, and both fathers and mothers reported more conflict with their sons. Much smaller differences were found among daughters.[1]

Had the Berkeley researchers started their study when the children were age fourteen, they surely would have found some differences between the adolescents from the 29 disrupted families and the adolescents from the 59 intact families. And they probably would have attributed these differences to the aftermath of the disruption, as most other researchers do. But because they could look back eleven years, they saw that some portion of the presumed effects of divorce on children were present well before the families split up.

Why is this so? It is, of course, possible that some children have behavioral problems that put stress on their parents' marriages. In these instances divorce, rather than *causing* children's problems, may be the *result* of them. But it is doubtful that inherently difficult children cause most divorces. The Berkeley researchers suggest, rather, that conflict between parents is a fundamental factor that harms children's development and produces behavioral problems. In many families, this conflict—and the harm it engenders—may precede the separation by many years.

There are many other characteristics of divorce-prone families that might affect children. For example, people who divorce are more likely to have married as teenagers and to have begun their marriages after the wife was pregnant. They also are less religious. It is possible that these families may provide a less stable and secure environment and therefore cause children more problems even while the family is intact. But no researcher would suggest that all of the effects of divorce are determined before the actual separation. Much of the impact depends on how the process unfolds after the separation and how the children cope with it. Nearly all children are extremely upset when they learn of the breakup. For most, it is an unwelcome shock. Judith Wallerstein and Joan Kelly found that young children seemed surprised even in families where the parents were openly quarreling and hostile.[2] Although young children certainly recognize open conflict—and indeed may be drawn into it—they usually can't grasp the long-term significance and don't envisage the separation. Moreover, parents typically don't inform their children of the impending separation until shortly before it occurs.

When children do learn of the breakup, their reactions vary according to their ages. Preschool-age children, whose ability to understand the situation is limited, are usually frightened and bewildered to find that their father or mother has moved out of the house. Preschoolers see the world in a very self-centered way, and so they often assume that the separation must be their fault—that they must have done something terribly wrong to make their parent leave. Three-year-old Sally promised never to leave her room a mess again if only Daddy would come home. Older children comprehend the situation better and can understand that they are not at fault. But they still can be quite anxious about what the breakup will mean for their own lives. And adolescents, characteristically, are more often intensely angry at one or both of their parents for breaking up their families.

SHORT-TERM ADJUSTMENT

The psychologists P. Lindsay Chase-Lansdale and E. Mavis Hetherington have labeled the first two years following a separation as a "crisis period" for adults and children.[3] The crisis begins for children with shock, anxiety, and anger upon learning of the breakup. (But as was noted, the harmful effects on children of marital conflict may begin well before the breakup.) For adults, too, the immediate aftermath is a dismaying and difficult time. It is especially trying for mothers who retain custody of their children, as about nine in ten do.

Helen, for example, faced the task of raising her two children alone. Even when she was married, Helen had taken most of the responsibility for raising the children. But Herb had helped out some and had backed her up when the children were difficult. Now responsibility fell solely on her. What's more, she was working full time in order to compensate for the loss of Herb's income. And all this was occurring at a time when she felt alternately angry at Herb, depressed about the end of her marriage, and anxious about her future. Harried and overburdened, she was sometimes overwhelmed by the task of keeping her family going from day to day. Dinner was frequently served late, and Sally and Mickey often stayed up past their bedtime as Helen tried to complete the household chores.

Children have two special needs during the crisis period.[4] First, they need additional emotional support as they struggle to adapt to the breakup. Second, they need the structure provided by a reasonably predictable daily routine. Unfortunately, many single parents cannot meet both of these needs all the time. Depressed, anxious parents often lack the reserve to comfort emotionally needy children. Overburdened parents let daily schedules slip. As a result, their children lose some of the support they need.

A number of psychological studies suggest that the consequences of the crisis period are worse for boys than for girls; but it may be that boys and girls merely react to stress differently.[5] Developmental psychologists distinguish two general types of behavior problems among children. The first—externalizing disorders—refers to heightened levels of problem behavior directed outward, such as aggression, disobedience, and lying. The second—internalizing disorders— refers to heightened levels of problem behaviors directed inward, such as depression, anxiety, or withdrawal. Boys in high-conflict families, whether disrupted or intact, tend to show more aggressive and antisocial behavior. Hetherington studied a small group of middle-class families, disrupted and intact, for several years. She found coercive cycles between mothers and sons, like the one between Helen and Mickey, to be prevalent. Distressed mothers responded irritably to the bad behavior of their sons, thus aggravating the very behavior they wished to quell. Even as long as six years after the separation, Hetherington observed this pattern among mothers who hadn't remarried and their sons.[6]

The findings for girls are less consistent, but generally girls appear better behaved than boys in the immediate aftermath of a disruption. There are even reports of overcontrolled, self-consciously "good" behavior. But we should be cautious in concluding that girls are less affected. It may be that they internalize their distress in the form of depression or lowered self-esteem. And some observers suggest that the distress may produce problems that only appear years after the breakup.[7]

It also is possible that boys do worse because they typically live with their opposite-sex parent, their mother. A number of studies report intriguing evidence that children may fare better if they reside with a same-sex parent after a marital disruption.[8] Families in which single fathers become the custodial parent, however, are a small and select group who may be quite different from typical families. Until recently, sole custody was awarded to fathers mainly in cases in which the mother had abandoned the children or was an alcoholic, a drug abuser, or otherwise clearly incompetent. Until there is more evidence from studies of broad groups of children, we think it would be premature to generalize about same-sex custody.

To sum up, researchers agree that almost all children are moderately or severely distressed when their parents separate and that most continue to experience confusion, sadness, or anger for a period of months and even years. Nevertheless, the most careful studies show a great deal of variation in the short-term reactions of children— including children in the same family. Most of this variation remains unexplained, although differences in age and gender account for some of it. Part of the explanation, no doubt, has to do with differences in children's temperaments. Some probably are more robust and better able to withstand deprivation and instability.[9] They may be less affected by growing up in a one-parent family, and they may also cope better with a divorce. In addition, clinicians have speculated that some children draw strength from adults or even peers outside of the household, such as grandparents, aunts, or close friends. But we are far from certain just how important each of the sources of resiliency is to the child's ability to cope with divorce.

LONG-TERM ADJUSTMENT

Even less is known about the long-term consequences of divorces than about the short-term consequences. Within two or three years, most single parents and their children recover substantially from the trauma of the crisis period. Parents are able to stabilize their lives as the wounds from the breakup heal. With the exception of some difficulties between single mothers and their sons, parent–child relationships generally improve. And the majority of children, it seems, return to normal development.

But over the long run there is still great variation in how the process of divorce plays out. Without doubt, some children suffer long-term harm. It is easy, however, to exaggerate the extent of these harmful effects. In their widely read book that reports on a clinical study of 60 recently divorced middle-class couples from the San Francisco suburbs and their 131 children, aged two to eighteen, Judith Wallerstein and Sandra Blakeslee paint a picture of a permanently scarred generation. "Almost half of the children," they write, "entered adulthood as worried, underachieving, self-deprecating, and sometimes angry young men and women."[10] Are these difficulties as widespread among children of divorce as the authors suggest? Despite their claim that the families were "representative of the way normal people from a white, middle-class background cope with divorce," it is highly likely that the study exaggerates the prevalence of long-term problems. Its families had volunteered to come to a clinic for counseling, and many of the parents had extensive psychiatric histories. Moreover, there is no comparison group of intact families; instead, all of the problems that emerged after the break-up are blamed on the divorce.[11]

We do not doubt that many young adults retain painful memories of their parents' divorce. But it doesn't necessarily follow that these feelings will impair their functioning as adults. Had their parents not divorced, they might have retained equally painful memories of a conflict-ridden marriage. Imagine that the more troubled families in the Wallerstein study had remained intact and had been observed ten years later. Would their children have fared any better? Certainly they would have been better off economically; but given the strains that would have been evident in the marriages, we doubt that most would have been better off psychologically.

Studies based on nationally representative samples that do include children from intact marriages suggest that the long-term harmful effects of divorce are worthy of concern but occur only to a minority. Evidence for this conclusion comes from the National Survey of Children, which interviewed parents and children in 1976 and again in 1981. For families in which a marital disruption had occurred, the average time elapsed since the disruption was eight years in 1981. James L. Peterson and Nicholas Zill examined parents' 1981 responses to the question, "Since January 1977 . . . has [the child] had any behavior or discipline problems at school resulting in your receiving a note or being asked to come in and talk to the teacher or principal?" Peterson and Zill found that, other things being equal, 34 percent of parents who had separated or divorced answered yes, compared with 20 percent of parents in intact marriages.[12]

Is this a big difference or a small difference? The figures can be interpreted in two ways. First, the percentage of children from maritally disrupted families who had behavior or discipline problems at school is more than half-again as large as the percentage from intact families. That's a substantial difference, suggesting that children from disrupted families have a noticeably higher rate of misbehaving seriously in school. (Although some of these children might have misbehaved even if their parents had not separated.) Second, however, the figures also demonstrate that 66 percent of all children from maritally disrupted homes *did not* misbehave seriously at school. So one also can conclude that most children of divorce don't have behavior problems at school. Both conclusions are equally valid; the glass is either half full or half empty, depending on one's point of view. We think that in order to understand the broad picture of the long-term effects of divorce on children, it's necessary to keep both points of view in mind.

The same half-full and half-empty perspective can be applied to studies of the family histories of adults. Based on information from several national surveys of adults, Sara McLanahan and her colleagues found that persons who reported living as a child in a single-parent family were more likely subsequently to drop out of high school, marry during their teenage years, have a child before marrying, and experience the disruption of their own marriages.[13] For example, the studies imply that, for whites, the probability of dropping out of high school could be as high as 22 percent for those who lived with single parents, compared with about 11 percent for those who lived with both parents, others things being equal. Again, the glass is half-empty: those who lived with a single parent are up to twice as likely to drop out of high school. And it is half-full: the overwhelming majority of those who lived with a single parent graduated from high school.

In addition, the NSC data demonstrate that children in intact families in which the parents fought continually were doing no better, and often worse, than the children of divorce. In 1976 and again in 1981, parents in intact marriages were asked whether they and their spouses ever had arguments about any of nine topics: chores and responsibilities, the children, money, sex, religion, leisure time, drinking, other women or men, and in-laws. Peterson and Zill classified an intact marriage as having "high conflict" if arguments were reported on five or more topics or if the parent said that the marriage, taking things all together, was "not too happy." They found that in 1981, children whose parents had divorced or separated were doing no worse than children whose parents were in intact, high-conflict homes. And children whose parents' marriages were intact but highly conflicted in both 1976 and 1981 were doing the worst of all: these children were more depressed, impulsive, and hyperactive, and misbehaved more often.[14]

To be sure, even if only a minority of children experience long-term negative effects, that is nothing to cheer about. But the more fundamental point—one that all experts agree upon—is that children's responses to the breakup of their parents' marriages vary greatly. There is no ineluctable path down which children of divorce progress. What becomes important, then, is to identify the circumstances under which children seem to do well.

WHAT MAKES A DIFFERENCE?

A critical factor in both short-term and long-term adjustment is how effectively the custodial parent, who usually is the mother, functions as a parent. We have noted how difficult it can be for a recently separated mother to function well. The first year or two after the separation is a difficult time for many mothers, who may feel angry, depressed, irritable, or sad. Their own distress may make it more difficult to cope with their children's distress, leading in some cases to a disorganized household, lax supervision, inconsistent discipline, and the coercive cycles between mothers and preschool-aged sons that have been identified by Hetherington and others. Mothers who can cope better with the disruption can be more effective parents. They can keep their work and home lives going from day to day and can better provide love, nurturing, consistent discipline, and a predictable routine.

Quite often their distress is rooted in, or at least intensified by, financial problems. Loss of the father's income can cause a disruptive, downward spiral in which children must adjust to a declining standard of living, a mother who is less psychologically available and is home less often, an apartment in an unfamiliar neighborhood, a different school, and new friends. This sequence of events occurs at a time when children are greatly upset about the separation and need love, support, and a familiar daily routine.

A second key factor in children's well-being is a low level of conflict between their mother and father. This principle applies, in fact, to intact as well as disrupted families. Recall the finding from the NSC that children who live with two parents who persistently quarrel over important areas of family life show higher levels of distress and behavior problems than do children from disrupted marriages. Some observers take this finding to imply that children are better off if their parents divorce than if they remain in an unhappy marriage. We think this is true in some cases but not in others. It is probably true that most children who live in a household filled with continual conflict between angry, embittered spouses would be better off if their parents split up—assuming that the level of conflict is lowered by the separation. And there is no doubt that the rise in divorce has liberated some children (and their custodial parents) from families marked by physical abuse, alcoholism, drugs, and violence. But we doubt that such clearly pathological descriptions apply to most families that disrupt. Rather, we think there are many more cases in which there is little open conflict, but one or both partners finds the marriage personally unsatisfying. The unhappy partner may feel unfulfilled, distant from his or her spouse, bored, or constrained. Under these circumstances, the family may limp along from day to day without much holding it together or pulling it apart. A generation ago, when marriage was thought of as a moral and social obligation, most husbands and wives in families such as this stayed together. Today, when marriage is thought of increasingly as a means of achieving personal fulfillment, many more will divorce. Under these circumstances, divorce may well make one or both spouses happier; but we strongly doubt that it improves the psychological well-being of the children.

A possible third key factor in children's successful adjustment is the maintenance of a continuing relationship with the noncustodial parent, who is usually the father. But direct evidence that lack of contact with the father inhibits the adjustment of children to divorce is less than satisfactory. A number of experts have stressed the importance of a continuing relationship, yet research findings are inconsistent. The main evidence comes from both the Hetherington and Wallerstein studies, each of which found that children were better adjusted. when they saw their fathers regularly. More recently, however, other observational studies have not found this relationship.[15]

And in the NSC, the amount of contact that children had with their fathers seemed to make little difference for their well-being. Teenagers who saw their fathers regularly were just as likely as were those with infrequent contact to have problems in school or engage in delinquent acts and precocious sexual behavior. Furthermore, the children's behavioral adjustment was also unrelated to the level of intimacy and identification with the nonresidential father. No differences were observed even among the children who had both regular contact and close relations with their father outside the home. Moreover, when the children in the NSC were reinterviewed in 1987 at ages 18 to 23, those who had retained stable, close ties to their fathers were neither more nor less successful than those who had had low or inconsistent levels of contact and intimacy with their fathers.[16]

Another common argument is that fathers who maintain regular contact with their children also may keep paying child support to their children's mothers. Studies do show that fathers who visit more regularly pay more in child support.[17] But it's not clear that they pay more *because* they visit more. Rather, it may be that fathers who have a greater commitment to their children both visit and pay more. If so, then the problem is to increase the level of commitment most fathers feel, not simply to increase the amount of visiting.[18]

These puzzling findings make us cautious about drawing any firm conclusions about the psychological benefits of contact with non-custodial parents for children's adjustment in later life. Yet despite the mixed evidence, the idea that continuing contact with fathers makes a difference to a child's psychological well-being is so plausible and so seemingly grounded in theories of child development that one is reluctant to discount it. It may be that evidence is difficult to obtain because so few fathers living outside the home are intimately involved in childrearing. It is also likely that, even when fathers remain involved, most formerly married parents have difficulty establishing a collaborative style of childrearing. We remain convinced that when parents are able to cooperate in childrearing after a divorce and when fathers are able to maintain an active and supportive role, children will be better off in the long run. But we are certain that such families are rare at present and unlikely to become common in the near future.

DOES CUSTODY MAKE A DIFFERENCE FOR CHILDREN?

The belief that the father's involvement is beneficial to children was an important reason why many states recently adopted joint-custody statutes. Supporters argued that children adjust better when they maintain a continuing relationship with both parents. They also argued that fathers would be more likely to meet child-support obligations if they retained responsibility for the children's upbringing. Were they correct? Joint custody is so recent that no definitive evidence exists. But the information to date is disappointing.

Joint *legal* custody seems to be hardly distinguishable in practice from maternal sole custody. A recent study of court records in Wisconsin showed no difference in child-support payments in joint-legal-custody versus mother-sole-custody families, once income and other factors were taken into account.[19] The Stanford study found little difference, three and one-half years after separation, between joint-legal-custody (but not joint-physical-custody) families and mother-sole-custody families. Once income and education were taken into account, fathers who had joint legal custody were no more likely to comply with court-ordered child-support awards than were fathers whose former wives had sole legal and physical custody. They did not visit their children more often; they did not cooperate and communicate more with their former wives; and they didn't even participate more in decisions about the children's lives. The investigators concluded that joint legal custody "appears to mean very little in practice."[20]

The handful of other small-scale studies of joint legal custody show modest effects, at most. It appears that joint legal custody does not substantially increase the father's decision-making authority, his involvement in childrearing, or the amount of child support he pays. Why is it so hard to increase fathers' involvement after divorce? For one thing, as we noted in Chapter 2, many men don't seem to know how to relate to their children except through their wives. Typically, when married, they were present but passive—not much involved in childrearing. When they separate, they carry this pattern of limited involvement with them; and it is reinforced by the modest contact most have with their children. Uncomfortable and unskilled at being an active parent, marginalized by infrequent contact, focused on building a new family life, many fathers fade from their children's lives.

Less is known about joint physical custody. But a few recent studies suggest that it isn't necessarily better for children's adjustment than the alternatives. Among all families in the Stanford Study in which children still were seeing both parents about two years after the separation, parents in dual-residence families talked and coordinated rules more; but they quarreled about the children just as much as did parents in single-residence families.[21] Several colleagues of Wallerstein followed 58 mother-physical-custody families and 35 joint-physical-custody families for two years after the families had been referred to counseling centers in the San Francisco area. Many of the parents were disputing custody and visitation arrangements. Children from the joint-physical-custody families were no better adjusted than children from the mother-physical-custody families: their levels of behavior problems, their self-esteem, their ease at making friends were very similar. What did make a difference for the children was the depression and anxiety levels of their parents and the amount of continuing verbal and physical aggression between them, regardless of the custody arrangement. The authors suggest that children whose parents are having serious disputes may have more behavior problems, lower self-esteem, and less acceptance by friends if they shuttle between homes. They are exposed to more conflict, and their movement back and forth may even generate it.[22]

The admittedly limited evidence so far suggests to us that custody arrangements may matter less for the well-being of children than had been thought. It is, of course, possible that when more evidence is available, joint custody will be shown to have important benefits for some families. As with father involvement, the rationale for joint custody is so plausible and attractive that one is tempted to disregard the disappointing evidence and support it anyway. But based on what is known now, we think custody and visitation matter less for children than the two factors we noted earlier: how much conflict there is between the parents and how effectively the parent (or parents) the child lives with functions. It is likely that a child who alternates between the homes of a distraught mother and an angry father will be more troubled than a child who lives with a mother who is coping well and who once a fortnight sees a father who has disengaged from his family. Even the frequency of visits with a father seems to matter less than the climate in which they take place.

For now, we would draw two conclusions. First, joint physical custody should be encouraged only in cases where both parents voluntarily agree to it. Among families in which both parents shared the childrearing while they were married, a voluntary agreement to maintain joint physical custody probably will work and benefit the children. Even among families in which one parent did most of the childrearing prior to the divorce, a voluntary agreement won't do any harm—although we think the agreement likely will break down to sole physical custody over time. But only very rarely should joint physical custody be imposed if one or both parents do not want it. There may be a few cases in which the father and mother truly shared the childrearing before the divorce but one of them won't agree to share physical custody afterward. These difficult cases call for mediation or counseling, and they may require special consideration. But among the vastly larger number of families in which little sharing occurred beforehand and one or both parents doesn't want to share physical custody afterward, imposing joint physical custody would invite continuing conflict without any clear benefits. Even joint legal custody may matter more as a symbol of fathers' ties to their children than in any concrete sense. But symbols can be important, and joint legal custody seems, at worst, to do no harm. A legal preference for it may send a message to fathers that society respects their rights to and responsibilities for their children.

Our second conclusion is that in weighing alternative public policies concerning divorce, the thin empirical evidence of the benefits of joint custody and frequent visits with fathers must be acknowledged. All of the findings in this chapter have implications for the way in which we as a society confront the effects of divorce on children. A question we will examine later is: Which public policies should have priority? What outcomes are most important for society to encourage and support? In some cases, such as the economic slide of mothers and children, the problem is clear, and alternative remedies readily come to mind. In other cases, the problems are complex and the remedies unclear. We will consider the difficult policy issues raised by the findings about the effects of divorce on children in Chapter 6.

First, however, we must note that a divorce does not necessarily mark the end of change in the family lives of children. A majority will see a new partner move into their home. A remarriage, or even a cohabiting relationship, brings with it the potential both to improve children's lives and to complicate further their adjustment. It is to the effects of remarriage on children that we now turn.

CHAPTER 5

Remarriage and Children's Well-being

In the late 1970s, only a handful of sociologists and psychologists had written about how children fared in stepfamilies. Fewer still had actually carried out studies of remarriage and stepfamily life.[1] The absence of attention to stepfamilies, one of the fastest growing family forms, was remarkable. Researchers behaved as though remarriage merely restored the simple nuclear family that divorce had broken apart.

But divorce and remarriage, especially when children are involved, fundamentally alter the way families work. Stepfamilies face unique problems for which there are not well worked out cultural solutions. Because Americans don't agree on how to conduct family relations within stepfamilies, cultural rules for stepfamilies to follow are vague or altogether lacking. Many stepparents find their responsibilities confusing, and many stepchildren are uncertain about what to expect from their stepparents.[2]

Researchers have come a long way in the last decade in revising and extending their understanding of stepfamilies. One recent review counted 95 dissertations on remarriage and stepfamilies, 600 professional research reports, and more than 135 popular books and articles written in the last decade.[3] Without doubt, more research is now published in a single year than was written in the entire decade of the 1970s. Moreover, stepfamilies have become more visible to the public. A 1989 special issue of *Newsweek,* entitled "The 21st Century Family," hardly mentioned old-fashioned nuclear families.[4] Instead, it devoted its first article to stepfamilies, describing them as a form of the family that we must learn to live with.

For a society almost entirely accustomed to nuclear families, the rapid growth of stepfamilies in the 1970s produced a cultural shock to our kinship system. To many observers, stepfamilies appeared exotic, if not bizarre, compared with garden-variety two-biological-parent households. Departure from the nuclear forms were automatically assumed to be an indication of inferiority. The evidence, in fact, suggests that many stepfamilies work quite well. Nevertheless, life in stepfamilies is more complex and often full of ambiguity. Remarriages may indeed be more fragile as a result. But everyone who has studied stepfamilies agrees that there is tremendous variation in the way that parents manage the transition from one marriage to the next. And, there is no simple generalization about how children fare in stepfamilies. In fact, stepfamilies are even less alike as a group than are nuclear families. Let's look at some of the reasons why.

WHO GETS COUNTED AS STEPFAMILY MEMBERS?

The first problem that comes up in describing stepfamilies is who gets counted as a stepfamily. It is not that easy to say when someone is a member of a stepfamily. Consider what happened when Herb remarried. He created a stepfamily that included his new wife, Alice, and her two children, June and Eddie. His own children, Mickey and Sally, lived with their mother but occasionally visited Herb and Alice's home. Does it then follow that Mickey and Sally, too, are part of a stepfamily? There is no rule for answering this question.

If the definition of a stepfamily is restricted to adults and children who reside in the same household, then a count can be made of stepfamilies. About one out of every five households containing a married couple with children under the age of 18 is a stepfamily.[5] This estimate is a cross-sectional snapshot. Children acquire and then sometimes lose stepparents in the course of growing up. Data from the National Survey of Children (NSC) suggest that at current rates of divorce and remarriage, close to a fourth of all children would spend some time living with a stepparent.[6] But if the definition of a stepfamily is expanded to include part-time stepparents and children

like Mickey and Sally, who see a stepparent at least occasionally, the proportion would rise.

This is the demographic reality of stepfamilies. But there is a psychological reality as well. Not everyone living in stepfamily households has a common definition of who's included in *their* family. Parents and children in the NSC were asked a simple question: "When you think of your family, who specifically do you include?" Although virtually all parents and children mentioned immediate biological relatives in their household (that is, parents, children, or siblings), some didn't mention stepchildren and stepparents in their household. Whereas just 1 percent of the parents neglected to mention a biological child in their home, 15 percent omitted a stepchild. And whereas 10 percent of the children did not list a biological parent in their household, a third left out a stepparent. These differences cannot be accidental. They reflect the fact that stepfamilies sometimes don't feel like families.

REAL PARENTS/STEPPARENTS

According to David Schneider, an anthropologist who has studied American kinship, our culture takes blood ties very seriously. The belief that a blood relationship cannot be ended or altered produces "a state of almost mystical commonality and identity."[7] It is as if blood relatives share a "natural substance" that cannot be taken away. In contrast, consider our sentiments about marital ties, the other main axis of American kinship. Without the natural substance, there is only a relationship, defined by law and custom, to bind relatives. We draw sharp distinctions between our blood relations and our relations by marriage—our spouses and our in-laws.

Stepfamilies contain an assemblage of family members, some related by marriage and some by blood. Notice how we distinguish them in common parlance. You would know exactly what it means if a friend of yours described her father in the following way: "He's my stepfather. I never knew my real father. He left home before I was ever born." A real father is the person who contributes half of your genetic material, but not necessarily the person who raises you from birth. These taken-for-granted cultural assumptions are one reason

why the notion of "stepparent" or "stepchild" often suggests a neglected or inferior substitute for the real thing.

Our legal institutions reenforce the second-class status of stepparents. David Chambers, a legal scholar, describes a case study of a family that experiences a series of disruptions.[8] The father leaves home and the children are raised by their mother and stepfather. When the mother dies some years later, the biological father, after a lengthy interval of no contact with his children, sues for custody rights of the children, who have been raised by a caring and involved stepfather. At the lower court level, the stepfather is permitted to maintain custody. Upon appeal, the higher court reverses the decision, deciding that the "real father" has prior rights to his children.

Child-support laws reflect the strong cultural norm that noncustodial biological parents, typically fathers, should support their children—even if they have never lived with them. On the other hand, stepparents, even if they live with their stepchildren for many years, incur no financial obligations if they move out of the home. Defined by law and custom, stepparenthood is seen as a special kind of fosterage with no enduring rights or responsibilities. The only legal recourse for stepparents who want to claim rights and responsibilities is to adopt their stepchildren, an act that seems to symbolize a deeper and more permanent tie, more like a biological relationship. As far as we know, no one has tried to count how often stepchildren are adopted by their parents.

Steprelationships, moreover, are frequently weak or ambivalent because stepfamilies can be battle grounds for parents inside and outside the home. Remarriage can produce rivalries between biological parents and stepparents that sometimes aggravate dormant hostilities between formerly married partners. Biological parents may feel supplanted and replaced. Stepparents may feel jealous of the biological parent's status as the "real" parent. In interviews conducted during the central Pennsylvania study, kinship terms were a big issue that symbolized struggles over family turf. Biological parents who wanted to cement ties between their children and their new partner sometimes encouraged the children to call their stepparent "Dad" or "Mom." Naming became a kind of political act, a way of realigning the family, as the following case illustrates.

Custodial Stepmother: I think she [noncustodial mother] is jealous of me . . . Now she just told me that I'm doing all the things that she should be doing, but she never thought of it until I started doing them . . .

Interviewer: So she feels that you are taking her place?

Custodial Stepmother: Yes. She has forbidden them to call me "Mom" when she's around. I am "Betty" and will never be anything else.

Interviewer: So they observe that rule, but when they are with you alone, what do they call you?

Custodial Stepmother: "Mom."

Interviewer: I mean you have no objection to their calling both you and her "Mom?"

Custodial Stepmother: No. I told them that they didn't have to call me "Mom" if they didn't want to. They could call me whatever they wanted to.[9]

Children were more likely to refer to their stepparents as Dad or Mom when they entered stepfamilies at younger ages or when they had little contact with their biological parent. Displaced biological parents were often upset when their children called their stepparents by kinship terms reserved for mothers and fathers. Children, however, had less difficulty with the notion that they had more than one father or mother. About two thirds of the children in the NSC who had active relations with their stepparents referred to them as "mother" or "father." If naming alone could be taken as a badge of membership, then most stepparents have been awarded a high degree of acceptance as family members.

STEPPARENT RELATIONSHIPS

But there are grounds for suspecting that a kinship term doesn't carry the same degree of sentiment when it is applied to a stepparent. The NSC contained a number of questions designed to measure the strength of ties among stepfamily members, compared with members of nuclear families. Stepchildren consistently expressed more negative descriptions of relations with their stepparents than did children in nuclear households with their parents. And stepparents who were raising both biological and stepchildren reported that stepparenting was more problematic and less rewarding.

This is not the whole story, however. The differences between reports from stepfamily members and nuclear family members were generally quite small. Most members of stepfamilies described life in quite positive terms that were not very different from the way that members of nuclear families described themselves. For example, when asked to describe the quality of life in their household over the past few months, 91 percent of the parents and 81 percent of the children in stepfamilies said that there was a large amount of sharing in their family; 78 percent of the parents and 66 percent of the children reported that relations were close; and 67 percent of the parents and children said that their family life was relaxed. Furthermore, children in stepfamilies and intact families supplied very similar descriptions of everyday life in their households—how often they did things with their parents, the rules around the home, how much say they had in decision-making, and how much they argued over rules. On the negative side, 30 percent of the parents and children in stepfamilies agreed that relations were tense, and 29 percent of the parents and 24 percent of the children in stepfamilies described their household as disorganized. The descriptions of nuclear family members were more positive, but the differences between them and stepfamily members were invariably small.

Nevertheless, other questions in the NSC suggested subtle, underlying differences in the quality of family life in step- and nuclear families. When asked to report about their stepchildren, close to half of the parents in the NSC who had both step- and biological children agreed strongly or in a qualified way that their stepchildren did not think of them as real parents, that it was more difficult to be a stepparent than a natural parent, that it was more difficult to discipline their stepchildren, that their children would have been better off if they had grown up with two biological parents, and that it was harder for them to love their stepchildren than their biological children.

Stepchildren concur that relations with their stepparents are not as rewarding. Compared with attitudes about parents among children living in intact families, stepchildren are far less likely to report that they feel close to a stepmother or stepfather. But children living in stepfamilies are just as likely to feel close to the biological parent that they live with as are children in nuclear families. It's the stepparent who is downgraded.

So when we scratch beneath the surface of family relations, the complexities of stepfamily life become more prominent. As often as not, stepparents and stepchildren remain in-laws. Their relations are derivative—they must rely on the good-will that they receive from being their mother's partner or their partner's children. It is almost as if biological parents were saying to their partners, "If you love me, you had better be nice to my children." And saying to their children, "If you love me, you had better be nice to your stepfather."

Sociologists like to distinguish between *ascribed* roles that are fixed by circumstances of birth and *achieved* roles that are earned by individual effort. Unlike the role of biological parent, the role of stepparent has an achieved dimension. Stepparents aren't treated like parents automatically; rather, their parental status must be earned. Stepparents are inclined to feel that their hard work is unappreciated. They sometimes resent having to earn the affections of their children-in-law. Still we must remember that not all stepparents feel this way. Close to half of the parents in the NSC did not admit to differences between biological and steprelations. Similarly, nearly half of all children reported that they felt quite close to their stepparents and wanted to be like them when they grew up.

THE ORGANIZATION OF STEPFAMILY LIFE

Stepfamilies are a curious example of an organizational merger; they join two family cultures into a single household. Of course, first marriages amalgamate family subcultures as well, but there is a difference. Couples in first marriages generally have a chance to work out their differences before children come along. And when children do arrive, they are usually eagerly anticipated by both parents. Stepfamilies, on the other hand, are not afforded the same amount of time to build a family identity; rather, it is frequently imposed upon them. Stepfamilies must blend subcultures that have been established for years. Children, steeped in the habits of an existing family culture, are often sensitive to the imposition of new family values, rules, and routines. Clinicians who have followed the adjustment of stepfamilies over time have frequently remarked on the difficulty of blending family cultures. Jamie Keshet, for example, comments that "working out a mutually acceptable concept of family may be more difficult than working out a definition of marriage."[10]

Keshet provides the example of a stepfather who arrives home to find the house a mess. His wife is in the kitchen preparing dinner while her son is nearby reading a book. He may be inclined to ask the child to help out but is unsure how his wife will react to such a request. She may, Keshet points out, feel angry because she believes that helping out isn't her son's role; or she may interpret her husband's request for participation as a criticism of her housework. Such a scene is less likely to occur in a nuclear family because the couple would have developed over time a common concept of how the family should operate.

Clinical researchers have attempted to chart the developmental process of establishing a common culture within the household. Patricia Papernow, among other clinicians, has discovered that stepfamilies typically go through a series of predictable stages on the way to developing a coherent family identity.[11] And because stepfamilies incorporate remnants of pre-existing family habits and histories, the task is different than in first marriages. To illustrate this point, let's return to the increasingly complex family situation of Helen and her children.

After nearly five years of sporadic dating, Helen finally entered a serious relationship with Lester, whose first marriage also had ended in divorce. Lester shares physical custody of his two sons with his former wife, JoAnn. As we look in on Helen again, she and Lester have been married for almost a year. They have experienced all the ordinary problems of forming a new household; and their situation is further complicated by Lester's two boys, whose busy schedules shuttling back and forth between houses absorb an enormous amount of the family's time and attention. Helen, full of visions of the Brady Bunch, initially tried to coax the boys into playing a more active role in her household. In her fantasy of establishing one big happy family, she hoped to make up to her children for the years of stress while she recovered from her divorce. Unfortunately, Lester's boys were not very cooperative. They were strongly attached to their own mother, who was keeping a watchful eye on Helen's efforts to incorporate her sons into the new household. To add to Helen's discomfort, Mickey was feeling intensely jealous of his mother's attention to the newcomers. And Sally, accustomed to the routines of single-parent life, felt displaced by so many outsiders.

Without providing a detailed description of the months of misunderstandings and injured feelings the family had to sort through, we can report that the chaotic state of family life was transitory. Lester, sensing that Mickey was feeling excluded, began to take the three boys out together and encouraged Helen not to be so critical of Mickey's understandable jealousy. As she let up, Mickey began to find his new family arrangement more rewarding. Now he especially appreciates having a father figure who is warm and supportive. Sally, on the other hand, continues to feel uncertain that she is better off in her new family. She spends a lot less time with Helen than before and blames Lester for her mother's more distant manner. Lester's efforts to win her over have not been notably successful. Sally rejects and feels excluded by the male members of the family and disdains the new male cultural emphasis on sports and outdoor activities. Sally has become more dependent and at the same time more withdrawn.

Our case study fits rather well with Papernow's description of the stages that many stepfamilies go through. She observes that a stepparent frequently starts out with fantasies of being a "healer"—a person who can miraculously knit a broken family back together by establishing strong bonds between the two sets of children. But the children often do not share these fantasies. The presence of the stepparent can be seen as an impediment to their unrealistic hope that their parents will get back together again.

The fantasy stage is often short-lived as members of the household struggle to form viable if not always gratifying relations. The early stages of stepfamily adjustment can either heighten the confusion or clarify the limits of family roles and boundaries. Stepparents quickly discover that they have been issued only a limited license to parent. Some, accepting and even appreciating the limits of their job description, draw back and bide their time. Others feel rejected and insist on trying to extend their mandate.

Ultimately, stepparents can play a constructive role in mobilizing family change and helping to establish a new set of shared understandings. Lester's willingness to draw Mickey into his family group helped to redefine the family boundaries, enabling the new family to coalesce. For parents and sometimes children as well, this redefinition may involve establishing greater psychological distance from former spouses and their relatives. It is a task that can threaten long-standing family habits or reminders of a former family life. For example, parents and children who have continued to spend holidays together, even though the parents are no longer married, may be forced to give up this arrangement when one or the other partner remarries.

To succeed in reorganizing the family, stepparents must be skilled diplomats who avoid competing with the other biological parent. They first must gain the support of their spouses and then await opportunities for acceptance by their stepchildren. According to Papernow, the mature stepparent is always placed in the role of an "intimate outsider," who can play a parent-like role but rarely can fill the place of the parent. The stepparent often becomes a special kind of adult resource for children—someone who is trusted because he or she is a peculiar kind of outside-insider in the family.[12]

Regardless of how skilled stepparents are, children will differ in their acceptance of the new family. Sally and Mickey, for example, had a variety of reasons for not feeling the same way about Lester. Researchers are just beginning to understand how individual differences in children's personalities, their relations to their parents, or their place in the family affect their responses to divorce and remarriage. It is clear, though, that children in the same family can have sharply different reactions to stepfamily life. And their reactions can affect not only their own development but also the stability of their parents' remarriage as well.

THE STABILITY OF STEPFAMILIES

It is an unpleasant fact that many stepfamilies do not survive the early stages of family reorganization. About one fourth of all second marriages dissolve within five years—a level of disruption that is significantly higher than the level among first marriages.[13] Scholars have interpreted the comparatively high rate of marital breakup in remarriages in different ways. Some believe that the absence of cultural guidelines and the added stress of building durable emotional ties to stepchildren make stepfamilies less stable. Many stepparents complain that having stepchildren in the home increases the tensions in their marriage. One study discovered that complex stepfamily households—such as those in which both partners have been married before and both have children—have a higher risk of breaking up.[14]

But even apart from the difficulties of managing the merger, remarried couples face somewhat higher odds of divorce. Couples in second marriages *without* children also have a higher risk of dissolution than childless couples in first marriages. This fact points to another reason for the high level of divorce in remarriages: People who have divorced once seem to be more prone to marital instability, although we do not know exactly why. Second marriers may have different beliefs about the acceptability of divorce and perhaps about the sanctity of marriage; they may have more psychological problems; they may be less religious and more unconventional; and they may tend to bring less capital into a marriage in the form of education and earning power. All these qualities place them at higher risk of divorce.

Still, the differences between couples in first and second marriages shouldn't be overstated. Overall, those who enter second marriages are only about 10 percent more likely to end their unions than individuals who enter first marriages. The differences are more conspicuous because remarried persons do not wait as long to leave an unhappy situation as individuals do in first marriages. The risk of divorce in remarriages is sharply higher in the first five years; but remarriages that survive longer than that are no more likely to end in divorce than are first marriages of the same duration.[15] We suspect that the stress of building a stepfamily makes it especially difficult for individuals who are more vulnerable from the start to remain married. In other words, both the complexity of stepfamily life and the predispositions of remarried individuals may lead to a somewhat elevated risk of divorce.

But before becoming unduly pessimistic about the prospects of stepfamilies, recall the evidence from the NSC presented earlier. Many stepfamilies appear to be functioning quite well. At least half of the stepfamilies in this national survey reported high levels of family satisfaction and close relations between stepparents and their children. True, the NSC excludes the families who did not manage to stay together. Still, it is encouraging to discover that so many of the stepfamilies that do survive can work out a satisfying existence. Like nuclear families, stepfamilies are hardly homogeneous. Life in stepfamilies can be confusing, ambiguous, and conflicted; but it also can be—and often is—harmonious and gratifying.

STEPFAMILY LIFE AND CHILDREN'S ADJUSTMENT

Having described the varied quality of stepfamily life, can we draw any general conclusions about whether the children of divorce are better or worse off if their parents remarry? Without consulting the data, it is easy to construct an explanation for why children might be better off when their parents enter a new marriage. First, the remarriage can bring a second earner into the family. A stepfather's income can reverse the economic slide that afflicts many divorced mothers and their children. Generally speaking, children in second marriages are almost as well off economically as children in first marriages.[16] Second, the addition of a new parent helps relieve the demanding existence of single parents. Someone else is around to share the burden of housework and the supervision of the children. One might anticipate, then, that children would benefit when their parents remarry.

But a counterargument can be made. Remarriage, as we have described, upsets existing family routines. It may renew or intensify hostilities between formerly married parents. The parent living outside the home may withdraw in reaction to it. Children may receive less attention from their custodial parent, who wishes to devote some attention to the new partner.[17] And stepparents are sometimes cast in ambiguous roles that prevent them from playing a constructive part in the family. All these conditions might lead us to predict that children will be worse off when their parents remarry.

Which of these competing explanations best fits the data? Neither, or perhaps both: It appears that children in stepfamilies have the same frequency of problems as do children from single-parent families. The NSC and the Child Health Supplement to the National Health Interview Survey (NHIS, also conducted in 1981) found that children in stepfamilies looked quite similar to children from single-parent families—and that both groups were not doing as well as children living with two biological parents.[18] For example, the parents of 10 percent of the children in the NHIS from both mother-stepfather and mother-only homes reported that their children had seen a psychiatrist or psychologist in the previous 12 months or that the parents had been told, or felt, that their children needed such help. In contrast, the parents of only 3 percent of the children from mother-father homes reported that their children had received or needed such help.[19]

Still, most children in stepfamilies are doing well. Consider the findings from a massive British survey, the National Child Development Study. As part of this study, nearly all of the 17,000 children who were born in Great Britain during the first week of March in 1958 were examined at birth and then reassessed at ages seven, eleven, and sixteen. At age sixteen, children living with stepparents were more likely to report conflict and to exhibit problem behavior of all sorts than were children living with natural parents, but the differences typically were modest. Elsa Ferri, reporting on this study, wrote that "the adverse findings related in every instance to a minority of the stepchildren; the great majority claimed to enjoy good relations with their stepparents, sibling conflict was the norm in *all* family groups and only slightly more in evidence among children with stepfathers."[20]

A number of observational, small-scale studies have found evidence that girls in mother–stepfather homes exhibit more problem behavior than do girls in single-mother homes, whereas boys show similar or reduced problem behavior in mother–stepfather homes.[21] In a two-year intensive study of 164 families, Hetherington and her colleagues found that both girls and boys in early adolescence (children who were eleven and one-half, on average, at the start of the study) had a particularly difficult time adjusting to the remarriage of their custodial parents. Early adolescent boys whose mothers remarried did not show the same level of improvement in behavior that many younger boys showed when their mothers remarried. The behavior of early adolescent girls sometimes deteriorated when a stepfather entered the family. Hetherington suggests that preadolescent girls often have an unusually close relationship to mothers who haven't remarried. The girls may view new stepfathers as competitors who disrupt this special relationship. The closer the relationship was between the mother and the new stepfather, the more conflict there was between the daughters and their mothers and stepfathers.[22]

But the national studies—which provide much more representative samples but rely on brief survey questions rather than intensive, first-hand observation—provide little evidence of sex differences.[23] So we are still in the uncomfortable position of not being able to draw definitive conclusions about when and why stepfamilies create enduring problems for children. It is tempting to advance an averaging theory of the effects of remarriage: there are some clear gains for children whose mothers remarry after a divorce (for example, larger family income) but some potential problems as well (for example, adjustment to the presence of a stepparent). This simple model, however, isn't very informative. When better studies that follow children over time are conducted, we would not be surprised to learn that some children's adjustment deteriorates when they enter stepfamilies while the adjustment of others improves. The aggregate results described above suggest that, overall, the number of winners and losers should be about even.

This much we do know: It seems likely that growing up in a stepfamily increases the risks of encountering problems relative to growing up with two biological parents but that, on average, the added risk is rather small. That the average risk is small is good news. It means that most children in most stepfamilies, like children in most divorced families, do not experience lasting problems. Nevertheless, it also suggests that under some circumstances, stepfamily life can create severe developmental damage. As yet, researchers have not answered the most interesting question—they have not identified which children or which family situations are the major source of the problems.

THE NEW EXTENDED FAMILY

We have already considered in this chapter how children's situations *within* the household change when their parents remarry. But remarriage changes the child's relations with kin in other households as well. Sociologists and anthropologists are just beginning to recognize the importance of divorce and remarriage for altering how Americans think about the extended family. For better or for worse, the high rates of divorce and remarriage seem to be changing the structure of American kinship—our universe of relatives and the sense of obligation we feel toward them.

Think once more about what happened to Mickey and Sally as a result of their parents' remarriages. When Herb curtailed contact with his children as a result of becoming involved in his second family, not only did Mickey and Sally experience his withdrawal but they saw a lot less of their father's family. The regular visits to their grandparents dropped off after their parents separated. It was really no one's fault: Helen was quite willing to host her former in-laws when they came to town, but their visits had never been frequent. Instead, the children had been accustomed to spending part of their summer vacation at their grandparents' lakeside home. These two-week trips were reduced to a few days when Helen drove them up herself. Her in-laws were cordial, but the visits were awkward; and it was clear after two or three days that it was time to leave. Herb's parents encouraged him to bring the kids along when he took his vacation with his new family, but somehow the arrangements never seemed to work out. Herb's wife, Alice, wasn't crazy about sharing the time with Mickey and Sally because she wanted Herb's parents to get to know June and Eddie. Besides, Sally was so demanding that the one time they had all gone together, she had nearly ruined the vacation.

No one was very happy about the declining contact between Mickey and Sally and their paternal grandparents. Herb's parents were very sad, Helen thought that it was unfair for the children to lose out, and Herb felt guilty. But under the circumstances, it was hard to avoid. The children did retain a strong relationship with

Herb's divorced sister and her children, who lived about an hour from their house. In fact, they saw their grandparents more at her house than at Herb's. She remained on close terms with Helen, even after Helen's remarriage. Herb felt that his sister sometimes sided with Helen and was fonder of her than of Alice. His sister denied this. But she did tell him that Helen was still her sister-in-law even though Herb was no longer married to her. And she claimed that she was related to Helen because she was after all the aunt of Helen's children. Herb wasn't prepared to argue with that.

Mickey and Sally certainly noticed that they saw less of their paternal grandparents. But their relations with Helen's parents became even closer. They continued to see their maternal grandparents once or twice a week even after Helen remarried. Helen's parents were fond of Lester, who they thought was extremely nice to their grandchildren. So they made a strong effort to involve his sons, their new stepgrandchildren, in their large and close family, especially after Mickey began to speak of his stepsiblings as his "brothers." The first Christmas, when toys had been handed out, Helen thought that Lester's boys had only received token presents. Embarrassed by her observation, Helen's parents outdid themselves the next year, giving grandchildren and stepgrandchildren twice as many gifts as they had the previous Christmas.

For his part, Lester was a vigorous advocate for his stepchildren in his extended family. He made sure that his four brothers and sisters got to know his two new children. His parents, who had no granddaughter, took a special liking to Sally. Remarkably, she actually felt more comfortable with them than she did with Lester. Helen was enormously grateful to her new in-laws for reaching out to both her children, and to Sally in particular.

We could go on to elaborate this story of an expanding universe of kinship ties. We did not mention Mickey and Sally's relationship with Alice's parents because it barely existed. Mickey did develop fairly strong ties with his stepbrothers' maternal grandparents. He often accompanied his stepbrothers to their mother's home. Lester's former wife, JoAnn, was perfectly happy to have Mickey come along. Her parents lived down the block, and Mickey became part of the family. JoAnn's parents even introduced him as a "grandchild-in-law." It began as a joke, but after awhile they and the rest of JoAnn's family did begin to think of him as a relative. That, of course, made Helen "a sort of relative," something like a distant cousin.

In 1970 Paul Bohannan described the elaboration of kinship ties after divorce as a "divorce chain."[24] More properly, it should be called a "remarriage chain."[25] Bohannan's point was that divorce and remarriage establish a complex network of potential relationships, only some of which become real relationships. As we noted earlier, Americans take blood ties very seriously. But they also construct kinship to suit their purposes. Schneider discovered, for example, that his divorced informants defined the kin of their former spouses as relatives if they *chose* to continue the relationship. Similarly, remarried persons defined their new in-laws as kin if they happened to develop a relationship. In other words, from the huge universe of potential kin, people actively create kin by establishing a relationship—by working at becoming kin. And they have wide latitude in choosing which links to activate. So Helen and her children are not in the least atypical of what happens after divorce and remarriage. If Mickey wants to consider his stepbrothers' grandparents as another set of grandparents, who is to say that he is misguided, especially if they in turn treat him like a grandchild? Some ex-in-laws—or "ex-familia," to use Colleen Johnson's term[26]—remain relatives and some new in-laws become relatives. Moreover, the universe of kin can be extended even further to individuals who are related only distantly through remarriage chains. Mickey became a grandchild-in-law to his stepbrothers' grandparents but Sally did not. So even within the same household, children will not necessarily agree on which individuals are members of their extended family.

This system may seem haphazard. In fact, the reshuffling of kinship ties after divorce often takes a predictable form: a decline in children's contact with their fathers' relatives and a strengthening of the ties to their mothers' relatives. We noticed this pattern in a national survey of grandparents that we conducted in 1984.[27] In stably married families children were equally likely to have strong ties with both sides of the family. In divorced families, however, children saw a lot less of their fathers' relatives because they saw a lot less of their fathers. And we observed that custodial mothers, like Helen, frequently relied on their kin to help out after the breakup. This assistance often resulted in a stronger bond between children and their maternal relatives, especially their maternal grandparents, than is found in families of first marriages.

The strong tie to maternal kin often persisted after remarriage, even when new ties were established with stepgrandparents. The number of stepgrandparents in our survey was small; but still we were impressed with how readily new bonds formed within these families, particularly when children were young at the time of the remarriage. As in Helen's and Herb's families, grandparents-in-law have a strong stake in developing ties with their new stepgrandchildren. By doing so, they solidify their relations with their new son- or daughter-in-law and retain access to their present or future grandchildren. Things don't always work out smoothly, however. Children are quite prepared to have multiple sets of grandparents, uncles, and aunts; but the middle generation can easily get caught up in conflict. Moreover, managing relations with so large a network of kin can be unwieldy.

As happened to Mickey, children in stepfamilies can find themselves enmeshed in a complex web of relationships with kin and quasi-kin. The tie that Mickey developed with the family of his stepfather's former wife is unusual, but children are exposed through remarriage to a wide range of adults who can under some circumstances become "family." Successive marriages expand the universe of relatives in much the same way that blood ties proliferate over generations. Whether these links significantly affect the development of children or their future life chances has not been systematically explored. Indeed, we know rather little about the way that children's lives are shaped by kin outside the immediate family.

Similarly, next to nothing is known about the enduring obligations of stepkin and quasi-kin. (For that matter, there is a limited stock of information even about kin related by blood.) So we can't answer some interesting questions. For example, if we were to study stepfamilies in their later years, would we find marked differences in the inheritances that parents leave to their biological and stepchildren? If so, would these differences carry over to the next generation?

Correspondingly, do adult children assume as much responsibility for their older steprelatives as they do for blood relatives?

These questions are of more than academic interest. The answers to them will determine how the new extended family functions as a system of exchange. Families not only nurture and protect children, they also distribute resources; and in so doing they create lasting obligations. Whatever else it may be, kinship is a set of rules for deciding how resources (emotional and material) are to be divided within and across generations. Remarriage has complicated this system of exchange because it offers no clear-cut guidelines for assigning rights and obligations.

Remarriage certainly expands the potential universe of kin, but does it also dilute the importance of each link? The potential value of weak ties to a large network of relatives shouldn't be underestimated. Access to information, to sponsorship, and to minor assistance through remarriage chains can have a significant impact on a child's life chances. But this thinner form of kinship may not be an adequate substitute for the loss of relatives who had a stronger stake in the child's success. Through divorce and remarriage, individuals are related to more and more people, to each of whom they owe less and less.

CHAPTER 6

Divorce, the Law, and Public Policy

Like Mickey and Sally most children are able to recover from the short-term trauma of divorce and resume normal development. Their mothers are able to get on with their lives, cope with being a single parent, and, in most cases, eventually remarry as Helen did. But the divorce often leaves scars. The standard of living of mothers and their children typically dips just after the breakup, and a complete economic recovery is unlikely unless and until the mother remarries. A remarriage, however, adds a stepparent to the family, an event that requires adjustment and can create new problems. Divorce, or the conflict that is usually a prelude to it, increases the risk to children of encountering problems later in life: dropping out of school, marrying and having children in the teenage years, and becoming divorced themselves. And whether or not they avoid long-term effects, children are likely to endure a wrenching period of upset and adjustment.

This is the experience that about four out of ten American children will face in the coming years. The concluding chapter considers what our society should do about it. Americans have viewed the family as a private sphere, beyond the reach of government. And yet we also recognize the need to intervene when necessary on behalf of children. It is in everyone's interest, for example, that children receive an education; consequently, parents are forbidden to remove their children from school before age sixteen. And our laws already regulate

(inadequately, it will be argued) the process of divorce. But should   **97**
we—can we—provide more public support to the institution of
marriage? Should we provide more direct public assistance to the
children of divorce? Should we try to restructure the way that men
relate to and support their children from previous marriages? These
are the questions we will examine in the remaining pages.

In a survey of divorce law in the Western world, the legal scholar
Mary Ann Glendon notes the paradox of the treatment of divorce in
the United States.[1] We have made it easier and quicker for individuals to obtain a divorce than any other country in the West except
Sweden. Yet our legal system and our public policies do less than
those in any other country to help families cope with the consequences of divorce. In granting a divorce to parents, we are liberal; in
assisting their children we are illiberal. Until recently, we did less
than any other country to ensure that absent fathers support their
children; yet we offer their children less public support. The result is
that American children face the worst of both worlds: more so than
children anywhere else, they cannot rely on either their parents or
their government to support them.

Until 1969, an American who wanted to obtain a divorce had to
prove in court that his or her spouse had done something so offensive
that the marriage should be ended. The list of common offenses
usually included adultery, abandonment, and physical or mental cruelty. It wasn't enough to tell the judge that the life had gone out of
your marriage or that you and your spouse didn't love each other
anymore or that one or both of you felt unfulfilled. To end the
marriage, one of you had to commit a terrible act. This legal standard
was adequate as long as most Americans strongly disapproved of
divorce and few obtained one. But as divorce became more common
and attitudes became more tolerant in the middle decades of the
century, couples increasingly sought a divorce simply because their
marriages had broken down. The divorce hearing became a sham, as
husbands and wives invented incidents or twisted their histories to
meet the conditions of the law.

It was in this context that support grew for allowing divorce on the
grounds that the marriage had irretrievably broken down, without
the need to prove that one spouse was at fault. Beginning with

California in 1969 and ending with South Dakota in 1985, all 50 states enacted laws that allow couples to request a divorce simply because of the breakdown of the marriage. The law in most states now requires that a divorce be granted after a separation of no more than a year, even if only one spouse wants the divorce and even if the other spouse isn't at fault. This short waiting period makes our divorce laws among the most lenient in the developed world. English law, in contrast, requires a five-year wait if one partner objects to the divorce. French law requires a six-year wait, and even then the court can deny a divorce if it would result in an exceptional hardship for an unwilling wife or her children.[2]

You might expect that a nation which makes divorce so easy would take steps to ensure that both divorcing parents continue to support their children. But the grim statistics on child-support payments in the United States contradict this notion. Only about half of all fathers who are ordered to pay child support pay the full amount, according to Census Bureau surveys of separated and divorced mothers. Moreover, the average amount awarded is modest and is rarely indexed to keep up with inflation. The states and the Federal government have done less to ensure that absent fathers provide an adequate amount of financial support than most Western European nations. In Sweden, where divorce also is easy and quick to obtain, the law sets a minimum amount that must be paid for support, and the government collects it from fathers with greater success than in the United States.[3]

There are two directions in which the law and public policy could move to correct this situation. One is to strengthen the bonds of marriage so that fewer couples would divorce. Were this direction promising, it would be the logical choice. But we will argue that public policy alone can do little to reduce the divorce rate. The other direction is to provide more aid directly to the children of divorce and to increase the support they receive from absent fathers. These two directions aren't mutually exclusive; our society could (and perhaps should) embark on both.

Before discussing them further, however, a potential dilemma must be addressed: do the two strategies work at cross purposes? Some observers, for instance, have argued that programs that have

ed him to earn their income. This division of labor encouraged
and women to work together to forge a family life. It was
ult to manage as a single parent, especially for women, whose
-market opportunities were limited. So divorce was a far less
tive option than it is today. Now it is possible, if still difficult,
woman to support herself and her children. Marriage is less of
onomic requirement than in the past.

rriage, in other words, used to be held together by more than
al affection and personal satisfaction. It also was held together
oral and economic constraints. Divorce is much more common
because those constraints are much weaker. The implication
ublic policy is that in order to strengthen marriage we would
to strengthen these constraints or create new incentives. But it
d be difficult to do so without imposing social costs few Ameri-
are prepared to pay—costs that would fall heavily on children in
-parent families.

nsider an extreme example. If our society really wanted to
e the divorce rate substantially at all costs, one sure-fire way
d be to enact a law forbidding women with preschool-age
en from working outside the home. Without doubt divorce
d drop dramatically because women no longer could support
selves and their children. But a law such as this would seem
d to most Americans. It would cause great suffering among the
ns of children already living in single-parent families. It would
ct the freedom of women in ways few Americans would accept.
t would remove from the workforce millions of workers on
employers and consumers rely. In fact, it is doubtful that any
f restriction on women's economic activities would be accept-
o the public. (Nor do we think it should be.) But without sub-
al restrictions, the economic independence of men and women
d hardly be altered.

ore realistic approach to strengthening marriage through eco-
measures would be to provide incentives that encouraged
e to get married and to stay married. But incentives large
h to be effective would be prohibitively costly. Consider recent
pts to encourage more births: several Eastern European na-
enacted policies that appear to have raised their birth rates

assisted single-parent families have eroded support for marriage.
According to this line of reasoning, improving the well-being of
single parents and their children, through cash assistance or better
enforcement of child-support obligations, has the unintended consequence of making it easier to leave a marriage. One could argue
similarly that programs that would provide support only to married
couples would put single parents at a disadvantage. Need we worry
about these unintended consequences?

Mary Jo Bane and Paul Jargowsky studied this question by examin-
ing the effects of various government policies on trends in marriage,
divorce, and childbearing over the past several decades. Their conclusion was that most policies had little effect at all—intended or unintended—on family structure. Even welfare payments, which frequently are blamed for the rise in female-headed families among the
poor, have no consistent connection with the trends. To be sure, the
number of female-headed families rose together with the value of
welfare payments in the 1960s and early 1970s, suggesting a linkage;
but the number of such families has continued to grow despite a
sharp drop in the inflation-adjusted value of welfare payments since
1975. The long-term trends in family structure, Bane and Jargowsky
argue, derive from major shifts in societal values and in the economy—changes so deep that no feasible government program can
easily alter them. (We will discuss these deep changes in the next
section.) They state: "Both conservatives and liberals should find this
analysis, if they believe it, troubling. Direct government policy is
neither the problem nor the solution, at least in terms of 'causing' or
'preventing' marital breakup and unmarried parenthood."[4] We agree
with this viewpoint. In order to understand why, it is necessasry to
examine in some detail the weakening that has occurred in the constraints that hold marriages together.

STRENGTHENING MARRIAGE

Much of what holds marriages together is the love and affection of
each partner for the other. Despite the high divorce rate, there has
been no decline in the importance that people attach to the personal
satisfaction they receive from their marriages. In fact, just the op-

posite has occurred: more and more, personal fulfillment has become the sole standard by which people judge their marriages. And this demanding standard can drive dissatisfied spouses to divorce. The consuming emphasis on self-fulfillment means that if your marriage is personally fulfilling, you will remain in it; but if it stops being fulfilling, there is little reason to continue. To the contrary, your friends and relatives, once they learn of your dissatisfaction, may even expect you to get a divorce. It used to be that people were hesitant to divorce solely on the grounds that they found their marriages personally unsatisfying; now, given the devaluation of other reasons for staying married, they almost have to.

The rise of personal fulfillment as the main criterion for evaluating marriages is due to two developments: the weakening of religious and other moral constraints and the demise of the breadwinner-homemaker family. As for constraints, the weakening has been part of a larger change in the way Americans view marriage. As recently as the 1950s, most people believed that marriage was the only proper status for adults; but now there is more tolerance of the unmarried and the previously married. A national survey in 1957 asked, "Suppose all you knew about a man (or woman) was that he/she did not want to get married. What would you guess he/she was like?" Half the sample responded that the person probably was deficient in some way, such as being sick, selfish, immoral, or neurotic. To be single in the 1950s was to be suspected of illness or bad character. But when a similar survey was carried out in 1976, only one third responded negatively; most were neutral.[5] Getting married is optional today. To be sure, a happy marriage is still highly valued, and most young adults still want to marry; but there is much greater acceptance of people who choose not to wed.

Similarly, there is a much greater acceptance of people who choose to end a marriage. At the very beginning of the book, we alluded to a study of changing attitudes toward divorce among a sample of mothers. In 1962 and again in 1977 the same random sample of young, white mothers from the Detroit area were asked whether they agreed or disagreed with this statement: "When there are children in the family, parents should stay together even if they don't get along." In 1962, 51 percent disagreed. But after fifteen years of witnessing,

and perhaps contributing to, a doubling percent disagreed. When asked the same cent disagreed.[6]

So by the 1980s there was a greater people who remained unmarried and of chosen to become unmarried. And the s to stay married had decreased. The incre married is part of a broader shift in valu world. During the past few decades, Wes greater value on personal satisfaction and person feels happy and fulfilled has becor standard for judging the worth of his or community. The political scientist Rona shift in Western values from an emphas such as food and shelter to an emphasi quality of life. He argues that the rising a about the shift because most people no satisfying their basic material needs.[7] thaeghe draws upon Inglehart's thesis b religious constraints and the rise of secu exact source, Americans, like most Weste the view that getting in and out of business, not the business of his or her fa

In the family realm, the shift toward panied by the greater economic indepe greater independence is itself the secon straints on divorce have weakened. As re about one out of seven married wom home; now the majority are. During th worked at all, they did so after their During the 1960s and 1970s, more children reentered the work force; an ment increased fastest among women now return to work within a year of th

As long as wives withdrew from t children, the roles of husband and w needed her to care for their children moderately at enormous expense. Czechoslovakia in the early 1980s provided three-child families with benefits amounting to half the average manufacturing wage. Yet Czech women were bearing about 2.1 children, on average, not much more than the 1.8 average in the United States and in England and Wales.[10]

It is not easy to devise incentives that might make marriage more attractive. In the past, the tax code has been the major mechanism for distributing benefits to families headed by a married couple. If we really wanted to underscore the importance of marriage, then perhaps we ought to provide greater tax relief in the form of tax credits to couples who are raising children. However, the merits of signaling our support for parents who stay together do not seem to outweigh a policy that further disadvantages single parents economically. Consequently, we cannot endorse such an arrangement. Reluctantly, we must conclude that tax policies are not the best instrument for conveying public support for marriage.

Some have argued that marriages could be strengthened by accepting the two-earner family and supporting it through better child care and a workplace that is more responsive to the needs of parents. Changes such as flexible working hours, paid leave for infant care, and subsidies for child care would indeed make life easier for working parents and improve the well-being of their children. We will argue in favor of such policies later in the chapter on just that basis. But it is doubtful that such changes would reduce the divorce rate significantly because they also would apply to single parents. While improving the quality of married life for working parents, the changes would also reduce the costs of leaving a marriage.

To truly encourage marital stability, a new policy must encourage husbands and wives to work collectively, to share family tasks. The workplace innovations don't necessarily do that. These reforms can create an environment that makes it easier for husbands and wives to share childrearing, but fathers may still resist. In Sweden, where both fathers and mothers are eligible for paid leave from work to care for infants, few fathers take the leave. One American study measured the effects on employees at two Federal agencies of rules that allowed them to start or end their working day a few hours earlier or later than the standard schedule. The authors found that almost everyone liked the flexible schedule and that it did allow working mothers to manage their child care and home responsibilities more easily. But fathers did not spend any additional time helping with child care. Instead, they used the flexibility to reduce commuting time, allow for recreational activities, and otherwise fit their work schedules to their existing personal life.[11]

We would argue, then, that it is unlikely that any feasible public policies could impose economic constraints or create economic incentives that would have a substantial impact on the divorce rate. But is it possible to strengthen moral constraints? To do so would require a strengthening of values such as responsibility to others, a greater sense of social obligation, and a devaluation of self-fulfillment. Such a strengthening would have to swim against the flood tide of individualism that has inundated the West. It could not be merely a call for a return to the 1950s family because married women are unlikely to leave the labor force in large numbers.

Some might think it impossible for such a sea change to occur, given the entrenched individualism of American culture. Social scientists have learned the hard way, however, that demographic trends can reverse direction unexpectedly. In the 1930s and early 1940s, every prominent demographer predicted that the U.S. birth rate would remain at the low levels of the Depression years. What occurred instead was the great baby boom of the period from 1945 to 1965. Americans turned inward toward home and family, perhaps in reaction to the hardships of the Depression and World War II. Young adults married at earlier ages than did any other generation before or since in the twentieth century. Although today's loosened economic constraints make another marriage boom unlikely, demographic surprises could await us later in the 1990s or after the turn of the century.

The strong attachment to marriage in the 1950s, however, had little to do with government—most politicians viewed the family as properly beyond their purview. Moreover, we would argue, with Bane and Jargowsky, that the rise in divorce and single-parent families in the 1960s and 1970s also had little to do with government. We doubt that an effort to strengthen marriage now would be successful unless it rose from the grass roots. It would probably take a social upheaval such as a prolonged economic downturn or a nation-wide religious revival to create a greatly renewed commitment to family ties. We should not expect much from the exhortations of officials unless their efforts resonate with broad social forces that are working to alter the moral climate from the bottom up.

Public attitudes became slightly less accepting of divorce in the 1980s. During that decade, the costs of divorce became more evident: the economic losses to women and children, the difficulties of joint custody, the emotional trauma for adults and children. In 1978, 42 percent of a national sample of adults agreed that divorce should be more difficult to obtain than it is now, whereas in a 1988 survey, 48 percent agreed. But this shift in sentiment is too small to bring about a large increase in Americans' commitment to remain in marriage. And even if we should see a more pronounced increase in sentiment against divorce, it doesn't necessarily follow that there would be a strengthening of marriage. To this point, it seems that recent apprehensions about divorce have encouraged more young adults to defer marriage and to live together instead.

In sum, we are skeptical that marriage bonds can be strengthened substantially by public policy, and we think a massive shift in popular sentiment unlikely. Although we would support public efforts to strengthen marriage, we are inclined to accept the irreversibility of high levels of divorce as our starting point for thinking about changes in public policy. The weakening of the economic and moral constraints on marriage means that there isn't much chance of returning to the relatively low divorce rates that existed before the mid-1960s. And even if our society were to return somehow to the rates of the mid-1960s, about one-fourth of all children would still experience a parental divorce.[12] A substantial proportion of all children will see their families break up in the 1990s and probably beyond. Our laws and our social-welfare programs must accommodate that reality. In particular, further action should be taken to reduce the harmful consequences of divorce on children. This will require direct assistance to the children and to their custodial parents—the second strategy which was noted earlier.

ASSISTANCE TO CHILDREN AND THEIR PARENTS

In Chapter 4 we attempted to discern what research tells us about why some children do better after a parental divorce than do others. This was a frustrating exercise: there are large gaps in the subject matter and uncomfortable inconsistencies in the findings. Reasonable people can read this literature and disagree about what it implies. Our reading led us to focus on two factors, namely, how well the custodial parent can function and how insulated the children are from continuing conflict between the ex-spouses. We have used these two factors to guide our thoughts about the kinds of changes in law and in social policies that would best assist the children of divorce.

Of the two, we believe that the more important factor probably is how effectively the custodial parent—usually the mother—continues to function after the breakup. We noted that the first few years are a time when parents understandably can feel intense anger, depression, or sadness. It is also a time when the standard of living of custodial mothers is likely to plunge because of the withdrawal of their husbands' incomes except for inadequate child-support payments. Mothers may have to move from the family home in order to divide their property with their former husbands. Under these conditions, it can be difficult for mothers to maintain the family's daily routine, from which the children could draw strength and support. It also can be difficult for them to provide the emotional support that their distraught children need. Upset and irritable, mothers and their children—especially their sons—can fall into cycles of bad behavior followed by harsh, inconsistent discipline, followed by more bad behavior. Yet custodial parents are the primary, and sometimes the only, remaining source of support for their children.

In addition, it is important to shield children from the continuing conflict, if any, between their parents. Children are harmed by intense conflict, whether or not their parents live together. Indeed, children who live in intact families with persistently high levels of conflict are the most distressed of all. In the initial period following the breakup, continuing conflict is very likely. Their love for both parents may cause distressing loyalty conflicts in children. The exposure to conflict may set a bad example that leads them to act aggressively or destructively later on. Their parents may use them as pawns or as go-betweens in the often angry negotiations surrounding a divorce. Public intervention should attempt to minimize children's exposure to conflict.

A third source influencing how children adjust to divorce is open to question: the importance of maintaining ties between the children and their noncustodial parents, usually their fathers. Although most observers, ourselves included, have believed that continued contact makes a difference in children's adjustment, the evidence in support of that assertion is mixed at best. As was noted in Chapter 4, some observational studies have reported that children adjust better when they have continuing contact with their noncustodial fathers. But other observational studies and large surveys have found that, other things being equal, the frequency of contact with fathers was not related to children's adjustment. Joint legal custody, which was supposed to increase fathers' visits, boost child-support payments, and reduce conflict between the parents, seems to have done none of the above. Moreover, there are hints that increased contact with the outside parent or joint living arrangements can prolong or even generate conflict between quarrelsome ex-spouses.

These negative findings about the importance of contact with the father have surprised and puzzled experts in the field. Perhaps the negative findings result from the low levels of contact that most divorced fathers maintain. Perhaps more sensitive measures of children's adjustment would find positive effects. Or perhaps what matters is not how many times children see their fathers but rather the quality of their relationship—a characteristic that is more difficult to measure. But the evidence from the National Survey of Children, as far as it goes, doesn't support this notion either. For now, we must conclude that the link between fathers' visits and children's well-being hasn't been convincingly demonstrated. Although we still advocate strengthening ties to fathers, we believe that public policy should place lower priority on this objective than on the previous two.

We have distilled, then, two principles for use in guiding public policy. We list them in order of importance:

1. The more effectively custodial parents can function, the better will be their children's adjustment.
2. The less parental conflict children are exposed to, the better will be their adjustment.

A third principle, which, in our view, is not as securely supported by research, is:

3. The more regularly children visit their noncustodial parents, the better will be their adjustment.

The order of these principles will be central to our argument because the principles can have conflicting implications. When that occurs, we will take support for the custodial parent and reduction in parental conflict as the primary goals, even if that means a reduction in contact with the noncustodial parent.

HELPING THE CUSTODIAL PARENT FUNCTION BETTER

An important way to help custodial parents meet their obligations at home and at work is to prevent the economic slide that typically occurs in the first few years following the breakup of a marriage. Toward that end, we urge further action to increase the amount of child support that is collected from noncustodial parents and to institute an assured child-support benefit for custodial parents. We also advocate changes in the workplace that would assist the parents of young children, whether married or not.

Child support. Until recently, the low levels of child-support payments and the lax enforcement of them were, as Lenore Weitzman argued, a "national disgrace."[13] Important but little-known changes in the law in 1984 and 1988, however, promise to take the United States out of the dark ages. The full effects of the changes won't be felt for several years. The 1984 law required that each state develop suggested guidelines for minimum child-support awards. These guidelines typically recommend that a certain percentage of the non-custodial parent's income be paid as child support, with the percentage increasing according to the number of children. The 1988 law requires that judges follow these guidelines in new child-support orders unless they write in the court record why they awarded less. The 1988 law also requires that child-support payments be withheld from paychecks immediately and automatically, just like payroll taxes. At first, automatic withholding will apply mainly to non-custodial parents whose children are receiving welfare. But starting in 1994 *all* new payments ordered or agreed upon will be subject to automatic withholding, no matter what the parents' income levels.[14]

If the state guidelines are fair and reasonable, and if the provisions are vigorously enforced by the states, these changes should significantly improve the standard of living of children of divorce (and of children born out-of-wedlock) by the end of the 1990s. But there are further steps that should be taken. The 1988 law requires courts to review awards in welfare cases every three years and adjust the award upward at the request of either parent if, for example, the non-custodial parent's income has increased. This provision should be extended eventually to all families.

More important, we urge that serious consideration be given to the creation of an assured child-support benefit, an idea developed by Irwin Garfinkel.[15] Under this plan, the state would set a minimum benefit level for custodial parents and their children who are supposed to receive child-support payments. If the absent parent paid less than the minimum, the state would make up the difference. The state, in turn, would strengthen its efforts to collect child support from absent parents. Garfinkel maintains that if the level of compliance with support orders could be increased substantially, then the share the state pays would be reduced, and the assured-benefit system would entail little additional cost. Given the current levels of child-support payments, there clearly is much room for improvement in compliance and collection. But no one expects that all noncustodial parents could be made to pay. Even if it involved moderate additional costs, the plan undoubtedly would boost the standard of living of many children in single-parent families who are presently living in poverty. Currently, Wisconsin and New York have Federal waivers to experiment with such a system, although only New York has begun to do so.

What effect would higher support awards and improved collection efforts have on the other desired outcomes, reduced conflict and continued contact with the noncustodial parent, which is usually the father? The new system could possibly increase conflict between some parents—if, say, fathers see their support burdens as unfair. But the impersonal mechanism of collecting support payments through wage and salary withholding means that the parents wouldn't have to interact with each other, not even to write or cash personal checks. In addition, fathers' contacts with their children might increase if their support payments are larger, although the evidence for this happening is at best only tentative. Nevertheless, if contact between non-custodial fathers and their children were affected at all, it would probably be in a positive direction. Fathers who pay more may feel entitled to see the children more frequently. And they might also acquire an enhanced sense of commitment to their children.

Workplace reforms. Easing the double burden of work and child care that many single parents face would be of great benefit to them and their children. Advocates of a "responsive workplace"[16] have argued that the conditions of work still are designed for workers who have wives at home during the day, which fewer men and no women have. Innovations such as flexible work schedules, leave for infant care, and part-time work with fringe benefits would alleviate some of the stress of daily life for employed, single parents. The innovations would therefore help them provide a supportive and predictable daily routine for their children. It seems likely that employers in the 1990s will be more responsive to the needs of parents. The young adults entering the labor force are in relatively short supply because of the sharp decline in the birth rate after 1965. So it will be in the self-interest of employers to attract and retain the labor of parents of young children. And it is in the interest of all who care about the upbringing of children to encourage such reforms.

A closely related need is for affordable, good-quality child care for working parents. A recent report on child care by a panel of the National Academy of Sciences found that the financial burden of paying for care falls quite heavily on single parents and parents with low incomes.[17] One study found that single mothers spent 17 percent, on average, of their weekly family earnings on child care, compared with 9 percent among mothers living with partners.[18] The high cost of care probably increases the use of unregulated, unlicensed providers both spend time with their children. Many fathers, perhaps a majority, fade out of their children's and their former wives' lives over the first few years after a divorce. But even among families in which fathers see their children regularly, few former spouses really cooperate in raising their children. In most cases the children live with their mother, except for occasional overnights with their father, and it is the mother alone who makes most of the decisions about the children's lives.

Instead of the shared, co-parenting style much heralded in articles about the new father, most couples engage in what we have called parallel parenting (if the fathers are involved at all). They don't consult much about what the children will be doing when with the other parent. In fact, they communicate as little as possible, pursuing instead two parallel tracks of parenting. It is an arrangement that minimizes both consultation and conflict. Most divorced couples simply aren't capable of the kind of continuous, courteous communication that is required if both of them are to play major roles in bringing up the children. The best that we should expect for most couples is parallel parenting that includes a modest amount of communication. Though not ideal, we should accept this style of managing parental responsibilities as a realistic arrangement that minimizes conflict.

Custody. In most divorces, custody is not an issue because it is taken for granted by both parties that the children will live with their mother. In the Stanford study, 78 percent of the parents agreed about the residential custody arrangements requested from the court. The outcome in seven out of ten of these uncontested cases was that the children lived with their mother; in another two out of ten they divided their time between both parents' homes; and in one out of ten they lived solely with their father.[22] So in most cases in which the parents agreed, the living arrangements lent themselves to a version of parallel parenting.

The great innovation in custody of the 1980s—in which California was the pioneer—was joint custody, which comes in two types: joint *legal* custody and joint *physical* custody. The argument usually given for joint legal custody is that by giving the father continuing who care for children in their homes—in "family day care"—or les expensive centers. The quality of care in these settings is quite vari able, but the price is right. Child-care assistance could directly benefi children of employed single parents by giving them the financia means to shop around for the best care for their particular child.

Mental health intervention. Apart from these economic and work-related issues, more custodial parents would benefit from more programs designed to ease their psychological adjustment to divorce. The model programs cited in the literature are designed to be preventive: admission is limited to newly separated adults. They rely mainly on group sessions, and they are designed to be short-term: after a period ranging from several weeks to several months, they end.[19] The focus is on general emotional support and on building competence in such areas as childrearing problems, legal and financial issues, and finding employment.[20] It is difficult to determine the effectiveness of these programs because few have been evaluated rigorously. But they do hold great promise for cushioning the impact of divorce for some of the adults who enroll in them.

More recently, clinicians have developed interventions for children, using a similar structure of group sessions lasting a fixed period of time. In one such program, nine-to-twelve-year-old children whose parents had divorced attended ten group sessions that covered topics such as feelings of isolation and stigma, disengaging from parental conflict, and the expression and control of anger.[21] As with the adult intervention, it is difficult to determine satisfactorily how effective the sessions have been, but they seem to have been helpful. We would encourage support for testing these interventions on broader populations in ways that can be rigorously evaluated. Should these limited interventions prove to be beneficial to a wide range of parents and children, they could become a valuable tool for managing the emotional upset of divorce.

REDUCING CONFLICT

While social scientists discuss how to reduce postdivorce conflict, millions of divorced couples have already done so by a simple method: they don't have much to do with each other, even if they authority over his children, the court increases the chance that he will choose to remain a part of their lives and will continue to help support them. But studies such as the Wisconsin and Stanford projects cited in Chapter 4 suggest that joint legal custody is failing to lure fathers into paying more child support or assuming greater childrearing responsibility. Overall, there seems to be little difference between a traditional award of sole custody to the mother with reasonable visitation rights for the father and an award of joint legal custody. In fact, it is striking how little difference there is in practice among any of the legal alternatives. Whether the standard is "the best interests of the child" doctrine or the "tender-years" doctrine or joint legal custody, most children live with their mothers after divorce, most decisions are made solely by mothers, and most fathers play a peripheral role in their children's lives.

On the basis of what we know about children's well-being, therefore, it is difficult to make a strong case that any of the alternatives is preferable to the other. The exact way in which legal custody (holding aside still the matter of physical custody) is determined is probably a secondary issue. Nevertheless, a preference for joint legal custody would reaffirm fathers' continued right to maintain an important role in the child's upbringing and would send a signal that fathers are expected to be responsible for their children even after a divorce. To be sure, the gesture would be largely symbolic—fathers with joint legal custody don't seem to act differently from those who don't have it. But it would provide a moral foundation for efforts to involve fathers in continued child care and increase the amount of child support they pay.

The determination of *physical* custody is of much greater importance for children. Under joint physical custody, children alternate between the mother's and father's residences according to an agreed upon schedule. It is a high risk/high payoff strategy. If successful, it can reduce conflict over who has custody and provide children with a continuing relationship with both parents. And it is the only form that encourages the shared, co-parenting style some think optimal. But it requires a great deal of communication and cooperation between the parents. Joint physical custody will merely prolong and deepen conflict between parents unless they can work well together.

Moreover, it assumes, contrary to the situation in most families, that the father wishes to share nearly equally the tasks of childrearing.

How many such couples now adopt and maintain joint physical custody is difficult to estimate. The Stanford study suggests that the proportion grew rapidly during the mid-1980s in northern California, but there is no other good source of information. If, as many observers believe, married fathers are becoming more involved in the care of young children, then a larger number of couples are likely to opt for this arrangement in the 1990s. We think, however, that it is easy to exaggerate the growth of involved fathers. So far, the change is hardly revolutionary. It is unlikely, we believe, that more than a small minority of couples will voluntarily choose joint physical custody. In nearly all other cases it would be a serious mistake to impose joint physical custody. The only exceptions would be the handful of cases in which both parents shared fifty/fifty—or even sixty/forty—in the childrearing but one refuses to agree to joint physical custody. For these few cases, mediation and special judicial consideration might be advisable.

For the majority of divorces, those in which one or both parents don't want joint physical custody, what, then, should be the standard for determining where the children shall live? There isn't enough social scientific evidence to point convincingly to any single answer. Personal values ultimately influence one's judgments. But we will make some observations based on our reading of the evidence.

Almost no one anymore advocates awarding physical custody solely to mothers on the grounds that they are inherently the better parents. The prevailing best-interest standard allows either parent to request sole physical custody, and it gives judges great discretion in making the award. In fact, its weakness is that it gives judges too much discretion. The uncertainty about how the judge will rule increases the potential for conflict in the minority of cases in which the parents disagree about custody or visitation. Moreover, the bargaining position of the husband usually is stronger than that of the wife. In most marriages the wife cares more about being with the children than does the husband. (Perhaps this isn't the way marriages *should be,* but we are asserting only that this is the way most marriages *are.*) And the husband has greater earning power than the wife.

Consequently, under the best-interest standard the husband can use physical custody as a bargaining chip. As the estranged spouses bargain in the shadow of the law, the husband can threaten to fight for custody (even though he doesn't really want it) in court unless the wife accepts a financial settlement favorable to him.

Mothers also can play this game. In the Stanford study, mothers and fathers were asked in an initial interview what form of physical custody they each wanted: sole mother, joint, or sole father. Then the researchers checked the court records to see what each parent had requested. Nine percent of fathers and five percent of the mothers had asked for more custody than they had said they wanted. (For example, they wanted joint custody but asked for sole custody.)[23] This is a small proportion of all parents (many more fathers, it turns out, had asked for *less* custody than they wanted) but a substantial proportion of parents in conflict-ridden cases. Other observers of the legal process claim that this bargaining tactic is not uncommon, although no hard evidence exists.[24]

It appears, then, that the best-interest standard has not changed the living arrangements of children very much—the overwhelming majority still live with their mothers. But in a small minority of cases its unpredictability may have increased conflict and bitterness between the former spouses and reduced the economic well-being of custodial parents and their children. Consequently, with respect to supporting the custodial parent and minimizing parental conflict, the best-interest standard—or probably any other standard that creates great uncertainty about how judges will rule—is a step backward.

In reaction to the flaws of the best-interest standard, significant support had developed among family law experts for a new primary-caretaker standard. David Chambers, for example, urges legislation that would instruct judges to award custody of young children to the parent "who has performed a substantial majority of the caregiving tasks for the child" that involve direct contact, such as "feeding, bathing, talking, snuggling, and so forth," unless the other parent can present "clear and convincing evidence that he or she is the more appropriate custodial parent."[25] West Virginia adopted a similar standard in 1981, and some version seems to be in use in a few other state courts.[26] To be sure, Chambers bases his recommendation primarily on psychological theories of the importance of attachment of young children to parents. But he also acknowledges the need to prevent custody from becoming a bargaining chip, and other advocates place more weight on this latter factor.[27]

Our preference for the primary-caretaker standard for physical custody rests on a belief that the less uncertainty there is about the likely legal outcome of a contested divorce case, the lower is the potential for conflict between the parents. If fathers and mothers both know to which parent a judge is likely to award custody in a case like theirs, neither can use the threat of litigation credibly to force concessions on other matters such as finances. In practice, of course, the primary caretaker is usually the mother, so most children would remain in their mother's physical custody, as is the case under the best-interest standard. It is possible that both parents will claim to have been the primary caretaker, or one parent will claim that the tasks were shared equally. When such disputes arise, however, it should be easier to demonstrate who has been the primary caretaker than who is "best" for the child's welfare. In terms of our principles, the primary caretaker standard for physical custody would help some parents function effectively (since fewer mothers would be pressured into accepting unfavorable financial settlements) and would reduce continuing conflict by decreasing the possibility of custody disputes.

Overall, our preference would be as follows. In most cases, legal custody ought to be retained jointly by both parents. In other words, no new determination of who is responsible should be made; rather, the legal responsibility should effectively stay as it was during the marriage unless there are compelling reasons to decide otherwise. As for physical custody, courts should allow joint physical custody when both parents freely choose it; but otherwise courts should assign children to live with their primary caretaker.[28] The outside parent should be allowed rights of frequent visitation, including overnight visits by the children.

Let us acknowledge again that we are not the first writers to recommend this course; Weitzman and Chambers, among others, make similar recommendations. Let us also acknowledge again that the empirical basis for choosing among these alternatives is still rather thin. In fact, the distinctions among all the legal standards seem to be modest; in all cases most children live with their mothers and most of their fathers will play a relatively small part in their upbringing. The contribution of the primary-caretaker standard for physical custody is that it minimizes the uncertainty about judges' rulings and reduces the bargaining leverage of parents who would trade custody rights for a more favorable financial settlement. The only real cost of this approach is that it places at a disadvantage the small number of fathers who shared roughly equally in the care of their children, wish to retain physical custody, but can't reach an agreement with their wives. As we've noted, these men may deserve special consideration. Courts might mandate mediation in these rare instances.

Mediation. Other steps should be taken to minimize the conflict between parents over the divorce settlement. Currently, parents are asked to come to an agreement at the worst possible time for negotiating—the immediate aftermath of the breakup of their marriage. It is no wonder that the negotiations are often acrimonious. During the 1980s, at least three states enacted statutes requiring that custody or visitation disputes be referred to a mediator before a court hearing can be held; other states allow judges to refer disputes to a mediator at their discretion.[29] Not enough is known yet about divorce mediation, but a number of studies suggest that it is a useful though imperfect tool for managing conflict. It appears that many couples with disputes, perhaps a majority, can reach satisfactory agreements in mediation and thus avoid the more adversarial atmosphere of the courtroom.

Mediation has its limits: Couples determined to maintain animosity usually succeed despite the best efforts of skilled mediators. Consequently, we are skeptical that it can enable feuding couples to become collaborative parents. But it appears that mediation services are able to help the majority of parents who wish to resolve their differences and get on with their lives. It has the potential to substantially reduce conflict between parents at the time of the divorce and subsequently; there is some evidence that parents who mediate their custody disputes are less likely to return to court later.[30] Its use should be encouraged.

FATHERS AND THEIR FAMILIES

The question still remains as to whether absent fathers can be helped to play a larger role in their children's lives. The efforts so far to encourage them to do so appear to be unsuccessful. To be sure, a small but growing number of largely well-educated, relatively affluent fathers are deeply involved in sharing physical custody of their children. But far more fathers still fade out of their children's lives. Half don't pay the full amount of child support they owe. Even an award of joint legal custody seems to change their behavior little. Why is it so difficult to change the behavior of absent fathers?

We think it is difficult because most fathers, whether absent or present, relate to their children primarily through their wives. For many men, in other words, marriage and parenthood are a package deal. Their ties to their children, and their feelings of responsibility for their children, depend on their ties to their wives. It is as though men only know how to be fathers indirectly, through the actions of their wives, who do most of the work of childrearing. If the marriage breaks up, the indirect ties between fathers and children also are broken. What is so radical about current attempts to involve absent fathers is that men are being asked to relate to their children directly—with no female intermediary. Men are to be encouraged through joint custody to play a direct role in rearing their children. This is a new strategy that must replace the entrenched father-through-mother-to-child pattern.

More fundamentally, we are struck by how little the underlying dynamic of parent–child relations has changed during the great rise in divorce. Our review convinced us that the most important factors in assuring the well-being of children after divorce are that the mother be an effective parent, providing love, nurturing, a predictable routine, and consistent, moderate discipline, and that the children not be exposed to continual conflict between the parents. If these conditions sound familiar, it is because they also are the same conditions that maximize the well-being of children in intact, nuclear families in which the mother does most of the childrearing. Perhaps we shouldn't be surprised that in divorced families, frequent interaction with the father seems to matter less for children's development than does an effective mother and an absence of conflict—the same probably holds true for most intact families. We may be attempting to engineer a direct role for fathers in divorced families that doesn't often exist in nuclear families. And if so, we shouldn't be surprised that the effort has had limited success so far.

If this line of reasoning is correct, then large-scale change in fathers' behavior is not likely to occur by simple modifications of custody orders or improvements in child-support enforcement—or, really, by any measures addressed solely to *absent* fathers. Rather, what may be required is a deeper and quite radical change in the way all fathers relate to their children. What may be needed is a greater sense of shared responsibility and partnership in childrearing. This does not imply a return to the "traditional" families of the 1950s, because 1950s fathers didn't share responsibility for childrearing; they left that to their wives. It implies, rather, a new bargain in which men and women recognize the worth of sharing both the breadwinning and the childrearing tasks.

Can it happen? If women's wages in the labor market approach men's, women may have more leverage in negotiating shared parenthood in exchange for pooling incomes. But equality in earnings will also make it easier to be a single parent. (And studies of two-career, upper-middle class marriages suggest that what wealthy, busy parents often do is hire a third person to do much of the childrearing and housecleaning.)[31] Perhaps the best that we can expect is a family system with unions that are more egalitarian but less stable. Such a system might provide an improvement in family life for adults, but it would not be a clear improvement for children.

This doesn't mean that we should abandon efforts to increase the involvement of divorced fathers in their children's lives. But for the near future, our chances of improving children's adjustment to divorce are probably better if we concentrate on supporting custodial parents and reducing conflict. More assistance to mothers and children and changes in family law carried out with those aims in mind will help the one million American children per year who must cope with their parents' divorce.

1. Divorce and the American Family

1. Arland Thornton, "Changing Attitudes towards Family Issues in the United States," *Journal of Marriage and the Family* 51 (November 1989): 873–893.
2. Lenore J. Weitzman, *The Divorce Revolution: The Unexpected Social and Economic Consequences for Women and Children in America* (New York: The Free Press, 1985); Lawrence Stone, *The Family, Sex, and Marriage in England, 1500–1800* (New York: Harper & Rowe, 1977); Edward Shorter, *The Making of the Modern Family* (New York: Basic Books, 1975).
3. Herman Lantz, "Romantic Love in the Pre-Modern Period: A Sociological Commentary," *Journal of Social History* 15 (1982): 349; Ellen K. Rothman, *Hands and Hearts: A History of Courtship in America* (Cambridge: Cambridge University Press, 1987); Frank F. Furstenberg, Jr., "Industrialization and the American Family: A Look Backward," *American Sociological Review* 31 (June 1966): 326–337; Carl Degler, *At Odds: Women and the Family in America from the Revolution to the Present* (New York: Oxford University Press, 1980).
4. William J. Goode, "The Theoretical Importance of Love," in Rose L. Coser, ed., *The Family: Its Structure and Functions* (New York: St. Martin's Press, 1964), pp. 202–219.
5. Ernest van den Haag, "Love or Marriage," in Coser, ed., *The Family*, pp. 192–201.
6. For a full discussion of this argument see Andrew J. Cherlin, "Postponing Marriage: The Influence of Young Women's Work Expectations," *Journal of Marriage and the Family* 42 (May 1980): 355–365.

7. Andrew J. Cherlin, *Marriage, Divorce, Remarriage* (Cambridge, MA: Harvard University Press, 1981).

8. Jessie Bernard, "The Good Provider Role: Its Rise and Fall," *American Psychologist* 36 (1981): 1–12.

9. Barbara Ehrenreich, *The Hearts of Men: American Dreams and the Flight from Commitment* (New York: Anchor Press, 1983); Elaine T. May, *Homeward Bound* (New York: Basic Books, 1988).

10. William L. O'Neil, *Divorce in the Progressive Era* (New Haven: Yale University Press, 1967); Lynn C. Halem, *Divorce Reform: Changing Legal and Social Perspectives* (New York: The Free Press, 1989); Mary Ann Glendon, *Abortion and Divorce in Western Law* (Cambridge, MA: Harvard University Press, 1987). Research suggests that the rise in divorce occurred prior to the legal changes, so that the new laws were more of a consequence than a cause of the increase in divorce. See, for example, Gerald C. Wright, Jr., and Dorothy M. Stetson, "The Impact of No-Fault Divorce Law Reform on Divorce in American States," *Journal of Marriage and the Family* 40 (August 1978): 575–580.

11. Gary Becker, *A Treatise on the Family* (Cambridge, MA: Harvard University Press, 1981); V. R. Fuchs, *How We Live* (Cambridge, MA: Harvard University Press, 1983).

12. Peter Uhlenberg, "Death and the Family," *Journal of Family History* 5 (Fall 1980): 313–320.

13. Peter Uhlenberg, "Cohort Variations in Family Life Cycle Experiences of U.S. Females," *Journal of Marriage and the Family* 36 (May 1974): 284–292.

14. Shorter, *Making of the Modern Family*.

15. John P. Gillis, *For Better, For Worse: British Marriages, 1600 to the Present* (New York: Oxford University Press, 1985); N. R. Hiner and J. M. Hawes, eds. *Growing Up in America* (Chicago: University of Chicago Press, 1985).

16. David Reisman, N. Glazer, and R. Denney, *The Lonely Crowd* (New York: Doubleday, 1950); Edgar Z. Friedenberg, *The Vanishing Adolescent* (New York: Dell, 1959); Paul Goodman, *Growing Up Absurd* (New York: Vintage, 1960).

17. Nicholas Zill and Carolyn C. Rogers, "Recent Trends in the Well-being of Children in the United States and their Implications for Public Policy," in Andrew J. Cherlin, ed., *The Changing American Family and Public Policy* (Washington, DC: Urban Institute Press, 1988), pp. 31–115.

18. Marie Winn, *Children without Childhood* (New York: Penguin Books, 1984), pp. 124, 134.

19. Little more than 10 percent of the marriages contracted in 1900 ended in officially recorded divorces. See Cherlin, *Marriage, Divorce, Remarriage*. And an unknown number of couples separated but did not divorce. Many of these divorces and separations, however, occurred to childless couples or to couples whose children had grown up. We know that today couples with young children are somewhat less prone to splitting up. (See Andrew J. Cherlin, "The Effect of Children on Marital Dissolution," *Demography* 14 (August 1977): 265–272.) If anything, the presence of young children probably was an even stronger deterrent to marital breakup at the beginning of this century. See also Samuel Preston and J. McDonald, "The Incidence of Divorce with Cohorts of American Marriages Contracted since the Civil War," *Demography* 16 (1979): 435–457.

20. Peter Uhlenberg, "Death and the Family," *Journal of Family History* 5 (Fall 1980): 313–320.

21. Larry L. Bumpass and James A. Sweet, "Children's Experience in Single-Parent Families: Implications of Cohabitation and Marital Transitions," *Family Planning Perspectives* 21 (November/December 1989): 256–260.

22. National Center for Health Statistics. Advance report of final natality statistics, 1987. Monthly vital statistics report, vol. 38, no. 3, suppl. (Hyattsville, MD: Public Health Service, 1989).

23. Bumpass and Sweet, "Children's Experience."

24. Frank F. Furstenberg, Jr., J. Brooks-Gunn, and S. Philip Morgan, *Adolescent Mothers in Later Life* (New York: Cambridge University Press, 1987).

25. Irwin Garfinkel and Sara McLanahan, *Single Mothers and Their Children* (Washington, DC: Urban Institute Press, 1986).

26. Frank F. Furstenberg, Jr., *Unplanned Parenthood* (New York: Free Press, 1976).

27. Kingsley Davis, ed., *Contemporary Marriage: Comparative Perspectives on a Changing Institution* (New York: Russell Sage Foundation, 1985); Andrew J. Cherlin and Frank F. Furstenberg, Jr., "The Changing European Family: Lessons for the American Reader," *Journal of Family Issues* 9 (September 1988): 291–297.

2. When Marriages Come Apart

1. George P. Murdock, "The Universality of the Nuclear Family," in Norman W. Bell and Ezra F. Vogel, eds., *A Modern Introduction to the*

124

Family (New York: The Free Press, 1949), pp. 37–44; David M. Schneider, *American Kinship,* 2nd ed. (Chicago: University of Chicago Press, 1980); Norman W. Bell and Ezra F. Vogel, eds., *A Modern Introduction to the Family,* rev. ed. (New York: The Free Press, 1968).

2. For an exposition of this idea, see Diane Vaughan, *Uncoupling: How Relationships Come Apart* (New York: Vintage Books, 1987).

3. Paul Bohannan, ed., *Divorce and After: An Analysis of the Emotional and Social Problems of Divorce* (Garden City, NY: Anchor Books, 1970).

4. Linda Thompson and Alexis J. Walker, "Gender in Families: Women and Men in Marriage, Work and Parenthood," *Journal of Marriage and the Family* 51 (November 1989): 873–893.

5. Rubin makes a strong argument for this explanation: Lillian B. Rubin, "Blue-Collar Marriages and the Sexual Revolution," in Arlene S. Skolnick and Jerome H. Skolnick, eds., *Family in Transition,* 5th ed. (Boston: Little, Brown and Co., 1986), pp. 177–192. See also Francesca M. Cancian, "Gender Politics: Love and Power in the Private and Public Spheres," in Skolnick and Skolnick, *Family in Transition,* pp. 193–204.

6. Graham Spanier and Linda Thompson have conducted one of the most informative studies of the divorce process: *Parting: The Aftermath of Separation and Divorce* (Beverly Hills, CA: Sage Publications, 1984).

7. For a full description of this study see Frank F. Furstenberg, Jr., Christine Windquist Nord, James L. Peterson, and Nicholas Zill, "The Life Course of Children and Divorce: Marital Disruption and Parental Conflict," *American Sociological Review* 48 (1983): 656–668.

8. William J. Goode, *Women in Divorce* (New York: The Free Press, 1956); Spanier and Thompson, *Parting;* for a review of this literature, see Sharon J. Price and Patrick C. McHenry, *Divorce* (Newbury Park, CA: Sage Publications, 1988).

9. Judith Wallerstein and Joan B. Kelly, *Surviving the Breakup: How Children and Parents Cope with Divorce* (New York: Basic Books, 1980), p. 14.

10. Janet R. Johnston and Linda E. G. Campbell, *Impasses of Divorce: The Dynamics and Resolution of Family Conflict* (New York: The Free Press, 1988), p. 8.

11. Goode, *Women in Divorce;* Spanier and Thompson, *Parting;* Lenore Weitzman, *The Divorce Revolution: The Unexpected Social and Economic Consequences for Women and Children in America* (New York: The Free Press, 1985).

12. Wallerstein and Kelly, *Surviving the Breakup,* pp. 38, 39.
13. Johnston and Campbell, *Impasses of Divorce.*
14. Hugh Carter and Paul C. Glick, *Marriage and Divorce: A Social and Economic Study* (Cambridge, MA: Harvard University Press, 1976).
15. Spanier and Thompson, *Parting.*
16. Robert R. Weiss, *Marital Separation* (New York: Basic Books, 1975); Bohannon, *Divorce and After;* Abigail Trafford, *Crazy Time: Surviving Divorce* (New York: Bantam Books, 1984); Vaughan, *Uncoupling;* Catherine Napolitane and Victoria Pellegrino, *Living and Loving after Divorce* (New York: Signet, 1978), p. 187.
17. Napolitane and Pellegrino, *Living and Loving,* p. 187.
18. Jessie Bernard, *The Future of Marriage* (New York: Bantam, 1972).
19. Thompson and Walker, "Gender in Families."
20. For a discussion of changing legal doctrines, see Lynne C. Halem, *Divorce Reform: Changing Legal and Social Perspectives* (New York: The Free Press, 1980).
21. Weitzman, *Divorce Revolution.*
22. Mary Ann Glendon, *Abortion and Divorce in Western Law* (Cambridge, MA: Harvard University Press, 1987). Glendon explains that the label "no-fault," which is somewhat misleading, was borrowed by journalists from the contemporaneous adoption by many states of no-fault automobile insurance.
23. Charles E. Welch III and Sharon Price-Bonham, "A Decade of No-Fault Divorce Revisited: California, Georgia, and Washington," *Journal of Marriage and the Family* 45 (May 1983): 411–418.
24. Eleanor E. Maccoby, Charlene E. Depner, and Robert H. Mnookin, "Custody of Children Following Divorce," in E. Mavis Hetherington and Josephine D. Aresteh, eds., *Impact of Divorce, Single Parenting, and Stepparenting on Children* (Hillsdale, NJ: Lawrence Erlbaum Associates, 1988), pp. 91–114.
25. James A. Sweet and Larry L. Bumpass, *American Families and Households* (New York: Russell Sage Foundation, 1987).
26. Robert H. Mnookin, Eleanor E. Maccoby, Catherine R. Albiston, and Charlene E. Depner, "Private Ordering Revisited: What Custodial Arrangements Are Parents Negotiating?" in S. Sugarman and H. Kay, eds., *Divorce Reform at the Crossroads* (New Haven: Yale University Press, 1990).
27. Weitzman, *Divorce Revolution;* Mnookin et al., "Private Ordering Revisited."
28. Judith A. Seltzer and Susan M. Bianchi, "Children's Contact with Ab-

sent Parents," *Journal of Marriage and the Family* 50 (1988): 663–677; Judith Seltzer, "Paternal Involvement after Divorce: The Father's View," forthcoming; Frank L. Mott, "When Is a Father Really Gone: Paternal–Child Contact in Father-Absent Homes," *Demography* 27, 4(1990): 499–517. Report prepared under Grant Number 1 R01 HD23160 with the National Institute of Child Health and Human Development, Center for Human Resource Research, The Ohio State University.

29. Terry Arendell, *Mothers and Divorce: Legal, Economic, and Social Dilemmas* (Berkeley, CA: University of California Press, 1986), pp. 112–113.

30. Arendell, *Mothers and Divorce*, pp. 116–117.

31. G. S. Rosenberg and D. F. Anspach, *Working Class Kinship* (Lexington, MA: Lexington Books, 1973); Claude S. Fischer, "The Dispersion of Kinship Ties in Modern Society: Contemporary Data and Historical Speculation," *Journal of Family History* 7 (1982): 353–375; Andrew J. Cherlin and Frank Furstenberg, Jr., *The New American Grandparent: A Place in the Family, A Life Apart* (New York: Basic Books, 1986).

32. Arendell, *Mothers and Divorce*, p. 106.

33. Wallerstein and Kelly, *Surviving the Breakup*, p. 29.

34. Eleanor E. Maccoby, Charlene E. Depner, and Robert H. Mnookin, "Coparenting in the Second and Fourth Years Following Parental Separation." Unpublished manuscript, Stanford University, 1990.

35. Eleanor E. Maccoby, Charlene E. Depner, and Robert H. Mnookin, "Coparenting in the Second Year after Divorce," *Journal of Marriage and the Family* 52 (February 1990): 141–155. We derived the estimate of one in six by multiplying the proportion of families in which the children saw their nonresident parent at least once every two weeks (two thirds) by the proportion of that group who had established a cooperative pattern of coparenting (one fourth).

36. Maccoby, Depner, and Mnookin, "Coparenting in the Second and Fourth Years Following Parental Separation."

37. Judith Wallerstein and Sandra Blakeslee, *Second Chances: Men, Women, and Children a Decade after Divorce* (New York: Ticknor & Fields, 1989).

38. Paul Bohannan writes about the helping professionals of the "divorce industry" in *All the Happy Families* (New York: McGraw-Hill Book Company, 1985).

3. The Economic Consequences of Divorce

1. This difference in family structure goes a long way toward accounting for the enormous racial disparity in poverty rates. To be sure, even within family types, black families are still poorer than white families; but the racial gap in poverty shrinks considerably when the marital status of the household head is taken into account. U.S. Bureau of the Census, Current Population Reports, series P-60, no. 166, *Money Income and Poverty Status in the United States: 1988* (Advance Data from the March 1989 Current Population Survey) (Washington, DC: U.S. Government Printing Office, 1989).

2. Greg J. Duncan and Saul D. Hoffman, "Economic Consequences of Marital Instability," in M. David and T. Smeeding, eds., *Horizontal Equity, Uncertainty, and Economic Well-Being* (Chicago: University of Chicago Press, 1985), pp. 427–470.

3. Greg J. Duncan and Willard L. Rodgers, "Longitudinal Aspects of Childhood Poverty," *Journal of Marriage and the Family* 50 (November 1988): 1007–1021.

4. Susan Bianchi and D. Spain, *American Women in Transition* (New York: Russell Sage Foundation, 1986).

5. R. H. Mnookin and L. Kornhauser, "Bargaining in the Shadow of the Law: The Case of Divorce," *Yale Law Journal* 88 (1979): 950–997.

6. Judith Seltzer and Irwin Garfinkel, "Inequality in Divorce Settlements: An Investigation of Property Settlements and Child Support Awards," *Social Science Research* 19 (1990): 82–111.

7. Lenore Weitzman, *The Divorce Revolution: The Unexpected Social and Economic Consequences for Women and Children in America* (New York: The Free Press, 1985).

8. James B. McLindon, "Separate but Unequal: The Economic Disaster of Divorce for Women and Children," *Family Law Quarterly* 3 (Fall 1987): 351–409; Charles E. Welch III and Sharon Price-Bonham, "A Decade of No-Fault Divorce Revisited: California, Georgia, and Washington," *Journal of Marriage and the Family* 45 (May 1983): 411–418.

9. U.S. Bureau of the Census, Current Population Reports, series P-23, no. 167, *Child Support and Alimony: 1987.* (Washington, DC: U.S. Government Printing Office, 1990).

10. C. S. Edwards, "Updated estimates of the Cost of Raising a Child," *Family Economics Review* 4 (1985): 26.

11. Greg J. Duncan and Saul D. Hoffman, "A Reconsideration of the Economic Consequences of Marital Dissolution," *Demography* 22 (November 1985).

12. Irwin Garfinkel, "The Role of Child Support Insurance in Anti-poverty Policy," *Annals,* AAPS, 479 (May 1985): 119–131; Irwin Garfinkel, "A New Approach to Child Support," *Public Interest* 75 (Spring 1984): 111–122.

13. Ann Nichols-Casebolt, "Economic Impact of Child Support Reform on the Poverty Status of Custodial and Noncustodial Families," *Journal of Marriage and the Family* 48 (November 1986): 875–880.

14. Nichols-Casebolt, "The Economic Impact of Child Support Reform."

15. Duncan and Hoffman, "Reconsideration of the Economic Consequences of Marital Dissolution"; Duncan and Hoffman, "Economic Consequences of Marital Instability."

16. Richard R. Peterson, *Women, Work, and Divorce* (Albany: State University of New York Press, 1989).

17. Richard V. Burkhauser and Greg J. Duncan, "Economic Risks of Gender Roles: Income Loss and Life Events over the Life Course," *Social Science Quarterly* 70 (March 1989): 3–23.

18. Ruth A. Brandwein, Carol A. Brown, and Elizabeth M. Fox, "Women and Children Last: The Social Situation of Divorced Mothers and Their Families," *Journal of Marriage and the Family* 36 (August 1974): 498–514; Robert S. Weiss, *Going It Alone* (New York: Basic Books, 1979); Lenore Weitzman, *The Marriage Contract* (New York: The Free Press, 1981); Sara McLanahan, "Family Structure and Dependency: Early Transitions to Female Household Headship," *Demography* 25 (1988): 1–16; Terry Arendell, *Mothers and Divorce: Legal, Economic, and Social Dilemmas* (Berkeley, CA: University of California Press, 1986).

19. K. Newman *Falling from Grace: The Experience of Downward Mobility in the American Middle Class* (New York: The Free Press, 1988).

20. Sara S. McLanahan, "Family Structure and Stress: A Longitudinal Comparison of Two-Parent and Female-Headed Families," *Journal of Marriage and the Family* (May 1984): 347–357.

21. James A. Sweet and Larry L. Bumpass, *American Families and Households* (New York: Russell Sage Foundation, 1988).

22. Weiss, *Going It Alone.*

23. Andrew J. Cherlin and Frank F. Furstenberg, Jr., *The New American Grandparent: A Place in the Family, A Life Apart* (New York: Basic Books, 1986).

24. Leigh A. Leslie and Katherine Grady, "Changes in Mothers' Social
Networks and Social Support Following Divorce," *Journal of Marriage and the Family* 47 (August 1985): 663–673.

25. Duncan and Hoffman, "Economic Consequences of Marital Dissolution."

26. McLanahan, "Family Structure and Stress."

27. Glen H. Elder, Jr., *Children of the Great Depression* (Chicago: University of Chicago Press, 1974).

28. There are few surveys that have tapped men's attitudes toward child support; but in those that have, men strongly endorse child support. Weitzman, *Divorce Revolution;* Ron Haskins, "Child Support: A Father's View," in Alfred J. Kahn and Sheila B. Kamerman, eds., *Child Support: From Debt Collection to Social Policy* (Newbury Park, CA: Sage Publications, 1988), pp. 306–327.

29. Robert I. Lerman, "Child-Support Policies," in Phoebe H. Cottingham and David T. Ellwood, eds., *Welfare Policy for the 1990s* (Cambridge, MA: Harvard University Press, 1989).

30. U.S. Bureau of the Census, *Child Support and Alimony: 1987*.

31. Janet A. Kohen, Carol A. Brown, and Roslyn Feldberg, "Divorced Mothers: The Costs and Benefits of Female Family Control," in George Levinger and Oliver C. Moles, eds., *Divorce and Separation: Context, Causes, and Consequences* (New York: Basic Books, 1979), pp. 228–245.

32. Arendell, *Mothers and Divorce*.

33. Weitzman, *Divorce Revolution*. See also Alfred J. Kahn and Sheila B. Kamerman, eds., *Child Support: From Debt Collection to Social Policy* (Beverly Hills, CA: Sage Publications, 1988).

34. Arendell, *Mothers and Divorce;* Weitzman, *Divorce Revolution*.

35. Arendell, *Mothers and Divorce*, p. 21.

36. Frank F. Furstenberg, Jr., and Graham B. Spanier, *Recycling the Family: Remarriage after Divorce* (Beverly Hills, CA: Sage Publications, 1984).

37. Frank F. Furstenberg, Jr., "Marital Disruption, Child Custody, and Visitation," in Kahn and Kamerman, *Child Support*, pp. 277–305.

4. Children's Adjustment to Divorce

1. Jeanne H. Block, Jack Block, and Per F. Gjerde, "The Personality of Children Prior to Divorce," *Child Development* 57 (1986): 827–840.

2. Judith S. Wallerstein and Joan B. Kelly, *Surviving the Breakup: How*

130

Children and Parents Cope with Divorce (New York, Basic Books, 1980).

3. P. Lindsay Chase-Lansdale and E. Mavis Hetherington, "The Impact of Divorce on Life-Span Development: Short and Long Term Effects," in David L. Featherman and Richard M. Lerner, eds., *Life Span Development and Behavior,* vol. 10 (Hillsdale, NJ: Lawrence Erlbaum Associates, 1990), pp. 105–151.

4. On children's needs from the family, see Eleanor E. Maccoby and John A. Martin, "Socialization in the Context of the Family: Parent–Child Interactions," in E. Mavis Hetherington, ed., *Handbook of Child Psychology,* vol. 4 (New York: John Wiley, 1983), pp. 1–101.

5. Chase-Lansdale and Hetherington, "The Impact of Divorce."

6. E. Mavis Hetherington, "Family Relations Six Years after Divorce," in Kay Pasley and Marilyn Ihinger-Tallman, eds., *Remarriage and Stepparenting: Current Research and Theory* (New York: Guilford Press, 1987), pp. 185–205. See also E. Mavis Hetherington, "Coping with Family Transitions: Winners, Losers, and Survivors," *Child Development* 60 (1989): 1–14.

7. Chase-Lansdale and Hetherington, "The Impact of Divorce."

8. For a review, see Robert E. Emery, *Marriage, Divorce, and Children's Adjustment* (Beverly Hills, CA: Sage Publications, 1988), pp. 85–86.

9. Hetherington, "Coping with Family Transitions."

10. Judith S. Wallerstein and Sandra Blakeslee, *Second Chances: Men, Women, and Children a Decade after Divorce* (New York, Ticknor & Fields, 1989). The families were offered short-term therapy in return for their participation in the research project. The well-being of the parents and children was assessed during the six-week therapy period, and they were reinterviewed eighteen months, five years, and finally ten years later.

11. The claim of representativeness is severely undermined by information found only in the appendix of Wallerstein's earlier book, co-authored with Joan Kelly, *Surviving the Breakup* (1980), which reported on the five-year follow-up. There the reader learns that the sample was referred to the divorce clinic for short-term therapy by lawyers, clergy, and occasionally court authorities. Families of children with severe psychiatric problems were excluded. But *parents* often entered the study with a long history of psychiatric problems. As Wallerstein acknowledges, half the men and close to half the women were "moderately disturbed or frequently incapacitated by disabling neuroses and addictions." Included in this group were the "chronically depressed"

and the "sometimes suicidal." And yet another 15 percent of the men and 20 percent of the women were "severely disturbed," with a long history of mental illness and a chronic inability to cope with the demands of life. Only a third of the sample were deemed to possess "adequate psychological functioning" prior to the divorce. We are never told what, if any, bearing parents' psychological histories had on their capacity to cope with divorce or to respond to the challenges of being a parent. It is hard to believe that their histories had no effect. It is also hard to believe that the parents in this study represent a typical sample of divorcing couples.

12. James L. Peterson and Nicholas Zill, "Marital Disruption, Parent-Child Relationships, and Behavior Problems in Children," *Journal of Marriage and the Family* 48 (May 1986): 295–307. By "other things being equal," we mean after statistical controls for the parent's education and race, the family's income, and the child's age.

13. Sara McLanahan, "Family Structure and the Reproduction of Poverty," *American Journal of Sociology* 90 (January 1985): 873–901; and Sara McLanahan and Larry L. Bumpass, "Intergenerational Consequences of Family Disruption," *American Journal of Sociology* 94 (July 1988): 130–152. McLanahan summarizes her research findings in the newsletter of the Institute for Research on Poverty at the University of Wisconsin: Sara McLanahan, "The Consequences of Single Parenthood for Subsequent Generations," *Focus* 11 (Fall 1988): 16–21.

14. Peterson and Zill, "Marital Disruption."

15. For a review, see Emery, *Marriage, Divorce, and Children's Adjustment*, pp. 89–90.

16. Frank F. Furstenberg, Jr., S. Philip Morgan, and Paul D. Allison, "Paternal Participation and Children's Well-Being after Marital Dissolution," *American Sociological Review* 52 (October 1987): 695–701. Frank F. Furstenberg, Jr., and Kathleen Mullins Harris, "The Disappearing American Father? Divorce and the Waning Significance of Biological Parenthood," paper presented at a Conference on Demographic Perspectives on the American Family, Albany, New York, 1990. See also Frank F. Furstenberg, Jr., and Kathleen Mullins Harris, "When Fathers Matter/Why Fathers Matter: The Impact of Paternal Involvement on the Offspring of Adolescent Mothers," in Robert Lerman and Theodore Ooms, eds., *Young Unwed Fathers* (Philadelphia: Temple University Press, forthcoming).

17. Frank F. Furstenberg, Jr., Christine Winquist Nord, James L. Peterson, and Nicholas Zill, "The Life Course of Children of Divorce:

Marital Disruption and Parental Contact," *American Sociological Review* 48 (October 1983): 656–668.

18. For an examination of the causal possibilities, see Judith A. Seltzer, Nora Cate Schaeffer, and Hong-Wen Charng, "Family Ties after Divorce: The Relationship between Visiting and Paying Child Support," *Journal of Marriage and the Family* 51 (November 1989): 1013–1031.

19. Judith A. Seltzer, "Legal Custody Arrangements and the Intergenerational Transmission of Economic Welfare," Working Paper 89-18, Center for Demography and Ecology, University of Wisconsin at Madison, July 1989.

20. Catherine R. Albiston, Eleanor E. Maccoby, and Robert H. Mnookin, "Joint Legal Custody: Does It Affect Nonresidential Fathers' Contact, Coparenting, and Compliance after Divorce?" *Stanford Law and Policy Review* 1(2) (1990): forthcoming.

21. Eleanor E. Maccoby, Charlene E. Depner, and Robert H. Mnookin, "Coparenting in the Second Year after Divorce," *Journal of Marriage and the Family* 52 (February 1990): 141–155.

22. Marsha Kline, Jeanne M. Tschann, Janet R. Johnston, and Judith S. Wallerstein, "Children's Adjustment in Joint and Sole Physical Custody Families," *Developmental Psychology* 25 (1989): 430–438; and Janet R. Johnston, Marsha Kline, and Jeanne Tschann, "Ongoing Postdivorce Conflict: Effects on Children of Joint Custody and Frequent Access," *American Journal of Orthopsychiatry* 59 (October 1989): 576–592.

5. Remarriage and Children's Well-Being

1. Paul Bohannan, ed., *Divorce and After: An Analysis of the Emotional and Social Problems of Divorce* (Garden City, NY: Anchor Books, 1970); Jessie Bernard, *Remarriage* (New York: Dryden Press, 1956); L. Duberman, *The Reconstituted Family: A Study of Remarried Couples and Their Children* (Chicago: Nelson-Hall, 1975).

2. Andrew J. Cherlin, "Remarriage as an Incomplete Institution," *American Journal of Sociology* 84 (1978): 634–650.

3. M. Ihinger-Tallman, "Research on Stepfamilies," *Annual Review of Sociology* 14 (1988): 25–48.

4. "The 21st Century Family," *Newsweek*, Winter/Spring 1990, Special Edition.

5. For variatious estimates, see Paul C. Glick, "Remarried Families, Stepfamilies, and Step Children: A Brief Demographic Profile," *Family Re-*

lations 38 (January 1989): 24–27, table 1; Larry Bumpass, "Children and Marital Disruption: A Replication and Update," *Demography* 21 (February 1984): 71–82; Sandra L. Hofferth, "Updating Children's Life Course," *Journal of Marriage and the Family* 47 (February 1985): 93–115.

6. Frank F. Furstenberg, Jr., Christine Nord, James L. Peterson, and Nicholas Zill, "The Life Course of Children and Divorce: Marital Disruption and Parental Conflict," *American Sociological Review* 48 (1983): 656–668.

7. David Schneider, *American Kinship*, 2nd ed. (Chicago: University of Chicago Press, 1980), p. 25.

8. David L. Chambers, "Stepparents, Biological Parents, and the Law's Perceptions of 'Family' after Divorce," in Stephen D. Sugarman and Herma Hill Kay, *Divorce Reform at the Crossroads* (New Haven: Yale University Press, 1991), pp. 102–129.

9. Frank F. Furstenberg, Jr., and Graham B. Spanier, *Recycling the Family: Remarriage after Divorce* (Beverly Hills, CA: Sage Publications, 1984), p. 113.

10. Jamie Keshet, "The Remarried Couple: Stresses and Successes," in William R. Beer, *Relative Strangers* (Totowa, NJ: Rowman and Littlefield, 1988), p. 36.

11. Patricia Papernow, "Stepparent Role Development: From Outsider to Intimate," in William R. Beer, *Relative Strangers* (Totowa, NJ: Rowman and Littlefield, 1988), pp. 54–82.

12. Papernow, "Stepparent Role Development."

13. James A. Sweet and Larry L. Bumpass, *American Families and Households* (New York: Russell Sage Foundation, 1987), table 5.12.

14. Lynn White and Alan Booth, "The Quality and Stability of Remarriages: The Role of Stepchildren," *American Sociological Review* 50 (October 1985): 689–698.

15. Sweet and Bumpass, *American Families and Households*, fig. 5.2.

16. Greg J. Duncan and Saul D. Hoffman, "Economic Consequences of Marital Instability," in M. David and T. Smeeding, eds., *Horizontal Equity, Uncertainty, and Economic Well-Being* (Chicago: University of Chicago Press, 1985), pp. 427–470; Elsa Ferri, *Stepchildren: A National Study* (Windsor, Berkshire: Nfer-Nelson, 1984).

17. Ferri, *Stepchildren*, p. 19.

18. For the NSC, see Paul D. Allison and Frank F. Furstenberg, Jr., "How Marital Dissolution Affects Children: Variations by Age and Sex," *Developmental Psychology* 25 (1989): 540–549. For the NHIS,

134

see Nicholas Zill, "Behavior, Achievement, and Health Problems among Children in Stepfamilies: Findings from a National Survey of Child Health," in E. Mavis Hetherington and Joseph S. Arasteh, eds., *Impact of Divorce, Single Parenting, and Stepparenting on Children* (Hillsdale, NJ: Lawrence Erlbaum Associates, 1988), pp. 325–368.

19. Zill, "Behavior, Achievement, and Health Problems."

20. Ferri, *Stepchildren,* p. 55.

21. See the following reports on small-scale, intensive studies by psychologists: James H. Bray, "Children's Development during Early Remarriage," in Hetherington and Arasteh, *Impact of Divorce;* Hetherington, "Family Relations Six Years after Divorce," in Kay Pasley and Marilyn Ihinger-Tallman, eds., *Remarriage and Stepparenting: Current Research and Theory* (New York: Guilford Press, 1987), pp. 185–205; Eulalee Brand, Glenn Clingempeel, and Kathryn Bowen-Woodward, "Family Relationships and Children's Psychological Adjustment in Stepmother and Stepfather Families," in Hetherington and Arasteh, *Impact of Divorce;* and J. W. Santrock, R. A. Warshak, C. Lindberg, and L. Meadows, "Children's and Parents' Observed Social Behavior in Stepfather Families," *Child Development* 53 (1982): 472–480.

22. E. Mavis Hetherington, "Remarriage, Lies, and Videotape." Presidential address to the Society for Research on Adolesence, Atlanta, March 23, 1990.

23. Two analyses of the NSC report that boys in stepfamilies showed fewer adverse effects than boys in single-parent families, though the differences were modest. The two analyses differ on whether girls fared worse in stepfamilies. See Paul D. Allison and Frank F. Furstenberg, Jr., "How Marital Dissolution Affects Children," and James L. Peterson and Nicholas Zill, "Marital Disruption, Parent-Child Relationships, and Behavior Problems in Children," *Journal of Marriage and the Family* 48 (May 1986): 295–307. An analysis of the 1981 Child Health Supplement to the National Health Interview Survey found no substantial differences between girls and boys: see Zill, "Behavior, Achievement, and Health Problems." And analysis of the British study found that boys in stepfamilies were faring somewhat worse than were girls in stepfamilies—the opposite of what the American studies suggest; see Ferri, *Stepchildren.*

24. Bohannan, *Divorce and After.*

25. Frank F. Furstenberg, Jr., "Remarriage and Intergenerational Relations," in R. W. Fogel, E. Hatfield, S. B. Kiesler, and E. Shanas, eds.,

Aging: Stability and Change in the Family (New York: Academic Press, 1981).

26. Colleen Johnson, *Ex Familia* (New Brunswick: Rutgers University Press, 1988).

27. Andrew J. Cherlin and Frank F. Furstenberg, Jr., *The New American Grandparent: A Place in the Family, A Life Apart* (New York: Basic Books, 1986).

6. Divorce, the Law, and Public Policy

1. Mary Ann Glendon, *Abortion and Divorce in Western Law* (Cambridge, MA: Harvard University Press, 1987).

2. Glendon, *Abortion and Divorce.*

3. Glendon, *Abortion and Divorce.*

4. Mary Jo Bane and Paul A. Jargowsky, "The Links between Government Policy and Family Structure: What Matters and What Doesn't," in Andrew J. Cherlin, ed., *The Changing American Family and Public Policy* (Washington, DC: The Urban Institute Press, 1988), p. 245.

5. Joseph Veroff, Elizabeth Douvan, and Richard A. Kulka, *The Inner American: A Self Portrait from 1957 to 1976* (New York: Basic Books, 1981).

6. Arland Thornton, "Changing Attitudes toward Family Issues in the United States," *Journal of Marriage and the Family* 51 (November 1989): 873–893.

7. Ronald Inglehart, *The Silent Revolution: Changing Values and Political Styles among Western Publics* (Princeton: Princeton University Press, 1977).

8. Ron J. Lesthaeghe, "A Century of Demographic and Cultural Change in Western Europe: An Exploration of Underlying Dimensions," *Population and Development Review* 9 (September): 411–436.

9. For a review of the trends and their connection to marriage and divorce, see Andrew J. Cherlin, *Marriage, Divorce, Remarriage* Cambridge, MA: Harvard University Press, 1981).

10. Michael S. Teitelbaum and Jay M. Winter, *The Fear of Population Decline* (Orlando, FL: Academic Press, 1985).

11. Halcyone H. Bohen and Anamaria Viveros-Long, *Balancing Jobs and Family Life: Do Flexible Work Schedules Help?* (Philadelphia: Temple University Press, 1981).

12. Larry L. Bumpass, "Children and Marital Disruption: A Replication and an Update," *Demography* 21 (February 1984): 71–82.

13. See Chapter 9, "Child Support: The National Disgrace," in Lenore J.
        Weitzman, *The Divorce Revolution: The Unexpected Social and Economic
        Consequences for Women and Children in America* (New York: The Free
        Press, 1985).
    14. The 1988 legislation was part of the Family Support Act of 1988, the
        welfare reform bill. For a brief summary see Andrew Cherlin, "Child
        Support: Now Everyone Will be Compelled to Pay," *Washington Post,*
        October 27, 1988. For a discussion of the 1984 Child Support En-
        forcement Amendments, see Irwin Garfinkel and Sara S. McLanahan,
        Single Mothers and Their Children: A New American Dilemma (Wash-
        ington, DC: The Urban Institute Press, 1986).
    15. See Garfinkel and McLanahan, *Single Mothers.*
    16. Sheila B. Kamerman and Alfred J. Kahn, *The Responsive Workplace:
        Employers and a Changing Labor Force* (New York: Columbia Univer-
        sity Press, 1987).
    17. Cheryl D. Hayes, John L. Palmer, and Martha J. Zaslow, eds., *Who
        Cares for America's Children* (Washington, DC: National Academy
        Press, 1990).
    18. Sandra J. Hofferth, "The Current Child Care Debate in Context," re-
        vised version of a paper presented at the Annual Meeting of the
        American Sociological Association, Chicago, August 1987.
    19. Robert E. Emery, E. Mavis Hetherington, and Lisabeth F. Dilalla,
        "Divorce, Children, and Social Policy," in Harold Stevenson and Al-
        berta E. Siegel, eds., *Child Development Research and Social Policy,* vol.
        1 (Chicago: University of Chicago Press, 1984), pp. 189–266.
    20. See, for example, Bernard L. Bloom, William F. Hodges, and Robert
        A. Caldwell, "A Preventive Program for the Newly Separated: Initial
        Evaluation," *American Journal of Community Psychology* 10 (1982):
        251–264; and Bernard L. Bloom, William F. Hodges, M. B. Kern,
        and S. C. McFadden, "A Preventive Intervention Program for the
        Newly Separated: Final Report," *American Journal of Orthopsychiatry*
        55 (1985): 9–26.
    21. JoAnne L. Pedro-Carroll and Emory L. Cowen, "The Children of Di-
        vorce Intervention Program: An Investigation of the Efficacy of a
        School-Based Prevention Program," *Journal of Consulting and Clinical
        Psychology* 53 (1985): 603–611. The researchers subsequently devel-
        oped a program for second- and third-grade children; see Linda J.
        Alpert-Gillis, JoAnne L. Pedro-Carroll, and Emory L. Cowen, "The
        Children of Divorce Intervention Program: Development, Implemen-

tation, and Evaluation of a Program for Young Urban Children," *Journal of Consulting and Clinical Psychology* 57 (1989): 583–589.

22. Robert H. Mnookin, Eleanor E. Maccoby, Catherine R. Albiston, and Charlene E. Depner, "Private Ordering Revisited: What Custodial Arrangements Are Parents Negotiating?" in S. Sugarman and H. Kay, eds., *Divorce Reform at the Crossroads* (New Haven, Yale University Press, 1990).

23. Ibid.

24. See Weitzman, *Divorce Revolution.*

25. David L. Chambers, "Rethinking the Substantive Rules for Custody Disputes in Divorce," *Michigan Law Review* 88 (1984): 477–569, pp. 562 and 538.

26. Glendon, *Abortion and Divorce.*

27. See Weitzman, *Divorce Revolution.* Glendon, *Abortion and Divorce,* p. 103, recommends that custody law "be modified to remove pressures on primary caretakers to give up needed financial resources because they fear losing their children."

28. Once again, exceptions might be justified for the very small number of cases in which the mother and father shared childrearing nearly equally but they cannot agree on physical custody. Here, no hard and fast rule can be proposed; mediation, counseling, and judicial discretion may be necessary.

29. Robert E. Emery and Melissa M. Wyer, "Divorce Mediation," *American Psychologist* (May 1987): 472–480.

30. Emery and Wyer, "Divorce Mediation."

31. See Rosanna Hertz, *More Equal than Others: Women and Men in Dual-Career Marriages* (Berkeley, CA: University of California Press, 1986).

INDEX

Academic problems. *See* School problems
Adjustment, children's, 62–76; short-
term, 65–67; custody and, 66, 73–76;
long-term, 68–70; factors in, 71–73,
75, 106–108; stepfamily life and, 88–
90
Adoption, of stepchildren, 80
Adolescents, 8–9, 65, 72, 89–90
Adults, long-term effects of divorce on,
69–70, 96
Alimony, 47, 57
Arendell, Terry, 37–38, 58, 59

Bane, Mary Jo, 99, 104
Behavioral problems, children's, 62–64,
66, 69, 72. *See also* Adjustment, chil-
dren's
Berkeley (CA) study, 63–64
Bernard, Jessie, 28
Birth rate, 102–103, 104
Blacks, 11, 12; and family disruption, 10,
14–15; and poverty, 45, 52, 53
Blakeslee, Sandra, 68
"Blended" families, 83–84. *See also* Step-
families
Block, Jack, 64
Block, Jeanne H., 64
Blood ties, 79, 93. *See also* Kinship ties
Bohannan, Paul, 19, 93
Boys: and coercive cycles, 63, 66–67; be-
havioral problems of, 62–64, 66; in
stepfamilies, 89–90

Bumpass, Larry L., 10, 11

Census Bureau, survey on child support,
57–58, 98
Chambers, David, 80, 115–116
Chase-Lansdale, P. Lindsay, 65
Child care, and working parents, 103–
104, 110–111
Child-care arrangements, parental, 28, 30,
33, 34, 103, 110–111. *See also* Parenting
Children, 9–12, 30; awareness of marital
difficulties, 21, 22–24, 65; and separation process, 22–24, 27–28; adjustment to divorce, 62–76, 88–90, 96,
106–108; in stepfamilies, 88–90. *See
also* Boys; Girls; Children of divorce
Children of divorce, 2, 7–12, 27–28, 40,
67, 106; life course of, 3, 9–12; effects
of economic decline on, 52–56, 106;
school problems of, 53, 56, 63, 69; behavioral problems of, 62–64, 66, 69,
72; adjustment of, 62–76, 88–90, 96,
106–108; and stepfamilies, 88–90;
public policy in support of, 98, 105,
106–118. *See also* Boys; Girls
Child support, 37, 47, 49–51, 57–61,
80, 98, 108–110; custody and, 73–74,
107; and public policy, 98, 105, 106–
108; reform in system of, 108–110
Coercive cycles, 63, 66–67, 71, 106
Cohabitation, 7, 11, 14–15, 76

139